COWING BRO
REAL ESTA
SHOE
UNITE
CIGARS
Coca-Cola

HOMEWOOD *Through the Years*

AURELIO'S
HARWOOD AVE
RIDGE RD
★HONORARY★ JOE AURELIO WAY

HOMEWOOD

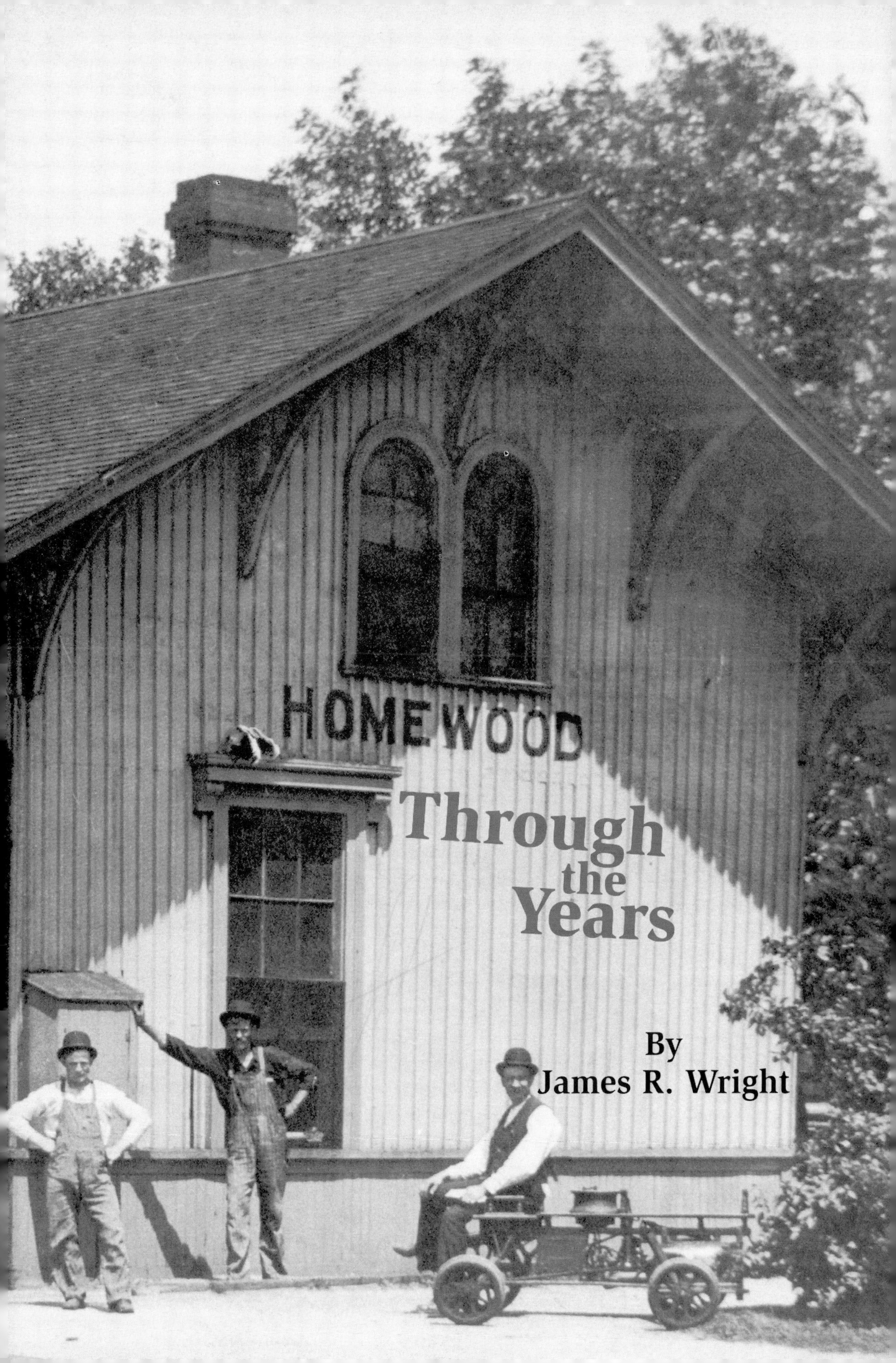

Through the Years

By
James R. Wright

The Donning Company Publishers
184 Business Park Drive, Suite 206
Virginia Beach, VA 23462

Steve Mull, General Manager
Barbara B. Buchanan, Office Manager
Pamela Koch, Editor
Lori Wiley, Senior Graphic Designer
Stephanie Danko, Imaging Artist
Mary Ellen Wheeler, Proofreader
Cindy Smith, Project Research Coordinator
Scott Rule, Director of Marketing
Travis Gallup, Marketing Coordinator

Ed Williams, Project Director

Library of Congress Cataloging-in-Publication Data
Wright, James R., 1959-
Homewood through the years / by James R. Wright.
p. cm.
Includes bibliographical references and index.
ISBN 1-57864-247-7 (hard cover : alk. paper)
1. Homewood (Ill.)—History. 2. Homewood (Ill.)—History—Pictorial works. 3. Homewood (Ill.)—Economic conditions. I. Title.
F549.H66W75 2004
977.3'1—dc22

2003027769

Printed in the United States of America at Walsworth Publishing Company

TABLE OF CONTENTS

PREFACE

Homewood Through the Years is the culmination of a lifelong interest in Homewood history. Over the last three years, much time has been spent intensively researching, interviewing residents, and gathering photographs for the publication of this book. As is the case with any project of this magnitude, a successful end result could not have been accomplished without the help and advice of a great many people. Although it is impossible to mention everyone who has helped with this endeavor, the assistance of many deserves special recognition.

First and foremost, I would like to thank the sponsors of this book, Joe Aurelio Jr. and Aurelio's Pizza and Ron Shropshire and the board of the directors of the Great Lakes Bank/Bank of Homewood. Without their financial support, the publication of this book would not have been possible. In addition, I would like to thank President Karen Smith and those on the board of directors of the Homewood Historical Society who supported and encouraged this project. Their cooperation in allowing access to their collections made researching and illustrating this volume much easier. All profits from the publication of this book will go to benefit the society.

In helping to research this book, the previous works of Adele Sandberg, Anna Adair, Mike Hinko, and historian Margaret Kuch have all served to provide a good foundation. Many thanks are also extended to Barbara Paul and the staff of the Chicago Heights Library whose microfilm collection of the *Star Newspaper* provided invaluable assistance. This collection was augmented by the collection of the *Dolton-Riverdale Pointer* newspapers, dating to 1906, at the Dolton Library; the newspaper collections, dating to the 1890s, at the Harvey Library; and the personal collection of James Pralle, whose bound editions of the *Homewood News* helped to fill in many gaps in the early history of Homewood. A special thank you is also extended to Village President Richard Hofeld, who allowed the author unfettered access to the records of the village of Homewood dating back to its incorporation in 1893.

In addition to these resources, the author is grateful to all who shared their reminiscences and recollections of Homewood, especially Garrett Tienstra, Florence Biesen, Tonetta Cowing Wehmhoefer, Norm Kranz, Tom Puhrmann, Jim Bannon, Jim Daanen, Ray and Dorothy Thomas, Clarence and Marge Baker, Sylvia and Dan MacMaster, and many more too numerous to mention.

For photographic assistance, much appreciation goes to the late John Dinges, whose efforts to collect historic photographs of Homewood back in 1976 serve as the foundation of the historical society's collection today and to Tonetta Cowing Wehmhoefer and the First Presbyterian Church, who graciously allowed the author access to their collection of photos from the Cowing family which date to the early years of Homewood. In addition, many photographs were obtained from the village of Homewood, the Homewood-Flossmoor Park District, and the *Star Newspaper* negative collection at the Chicago Heights Library. These institutions and countless individuals, like Donald Paden, Jean Mackenzie, William F. Moore, Gloria Sublette, Doris Waldschmidt, Dixie Mitchell, Jean Ratko, Susan White, Peggy Burns, Don Steiner, Bert Heuer, George Boggs, and the Meyer Estate, and many more individuals listed in the photo credits, provided most of the interesting photographs included in this volume. Without their help and the help of Bert Heuer, who made loan of his extensive negative collection, Carolyn Funk, who took many of the present-day photos gracing the final chapters, and Sarah Serviss, who digitally touched up some of the older photographs, this book would not be as visually appealing as it is. Special thanks are also extended to Frank Casella who took the author's photo and to Chet Chylinski for taking photos for the book cover. Photos not credited are from the Homewood Historical Society or the author's collections.

Many thanks are also extended to Dick Condon, Mary McDermed, Karen Smith, and Ted Bertrand who reviewed parts or all of the manuscript and offered advice and counsel and to Kris Condon who reviewed the manuscript and also was a great help with computer "issues." I would like to also thank the staff at The Donning Company Publishers for all their help and patience.

Finally, I would conclude by saying that while all attempts have been made to meticulously research this book, there are bound to be some errors and omissions. For these, I apologize and take complete responsibility. Historical research is a continuous process, and new information is uncovered all the time. Readers are encouraged to send their recollections, corrections, and photographs portraying Homewood scenes and personalities to the author in care of the Homewood Historical Society, P.O. Box 1144, Homewood, Illinois 60430.

James R. Wright

Joliet and Marquette exploring Illinois waters

CHAPTER 1
The Earliest Settlers

Driving through Homewood and surrounding suburbs today, it is hard to imagine what the area looked like two hundred, one hundred, or even fifty years ago. At every turn, housing subdivisions and shopping centers dominate the view. With each passing year, more and more vacant land has given way to our insatiable appetite for development, making it hard to remember what some areas looked like even ten years ago. The landscape that greeted the first European explorers, however, was infinitely different than what we see each day.

French Jesuit missionary Jacques Marquette and fur trader Louis Joliet were the first Europeans known to enter the Illinois country, as the area of the present-day state was known in the seventeenth and eighteenth centuries. In 1673, Marquette and Joliet journeyed down the Mississippi River along the western boundary of Illinois. On their return trip north, they traveled up the Illinois River and along its tributary, the Des Plaines River. The men and their crew easily portaged or carried their small boats between the Des Plaines River and the Chicago River, which flowed directly into Lake Michigan. Marquette and Joliet found this part of Illinois to be lush country, full of game, including buffalo, with gently rolling prairies, forested savannas, and water as clear as crystal. Their discovery of the Chicago portage, as it was later called, became an important link in the trade routes between the Great Lakes, the Mississippi River, and the bountiful lands in between we know as Illinois.

Missionary and explorer Father Jacques Marquette

During their journey, Marquette and Joliet also encountered the Illiniwek, a confederation of Algonquin-speaking tribes that had banded together as one nation. The Illiniwek, or Illinois to the French, were peaceable, hardworking, and friendly to the explorers. So receptive were the native peoples, Marquette later returned to the Illinois country in 1674 to establish a mission among the Kaskaskia tribe of the Illiniwek. Following in Marquette's footsteps, other Frenchmen came to the area, and, with the cooperation of the friendly native peoples, the French established a fur trade that quickly flourished.

For almost a century, the French remained in control of the Illinois country, which was a part of the French territory called Louisiana. After engaging in a series of conflicts with the British to gain control over the North American continent, the French eventually ceded all Louisiana Territory lands east of the Mississippi to the British under the Treaty of Paris in 1763. During this period of French and British warfare, the Indian peoples also fought amongst themselves. By 1765, the Illinois people had been decimated by disease and intertribal warfare. Other tribes, including the Iroquois, Sac (Sauk), Fox, Miami, and Potawatomi took possession of the Illinois lands. The Potawatomi dominated and were in control at the end of the Revolutionary War when American settlers gradually began to move westward.

From the beginning of westward expansion, the Potawatomi were hostile to the settlers. Unlike the French, the Americans built permanent settlements. They cut down the forests to clear land for farming and in doing so destroyed Native American hunting grounds and pushed the Native Americans from lands they had lived on for hundreds of years. Tensions developed that led to sporadic attacks by the Indians on the scattered settlers throughout the region. Because of

View of Fort Dearborn from Lake Michigan

these attacks, settlement proceeded slowly in Illinois and was concentrated in the southern sections of the territory. The first settlement in northern Illinois was developed around Fort Dearborn, which the United States government built in 1803 near the mouth of the Chicago River along Lake Michigan. Here settlers could seek shelter whenever there was danger of an Indian attack. It was near Fort Dearborn that one of the most infamous of these attacks occurred.

Burning of Fort Dearborn

With the advent of the War of 1812, the Indians sided with the British, and their combined forces posed a great threat to the troops garrisoned at the fort and the settlers in the surrounding area. In the summer of 1812, Captain Nathan Heald, commander of the fort, was ordered to evacuate it and proceed with his troops to the safety of Fort Wayne. After destroying all ammunition that could not be carried with them, a procession of about one hundred soldiers, settlers, and friendly Indian guides left the fort on August 15, 1812. Several miles from the fort, the group was attacked by a band of about five hundred Potawatomi and allied Indians. Half of the group of soldiers and settlers were killed, and the remaining survivors were taken captive in what became known as the Fort Dearborn Massacre. Fort Dearborn itself was pillaged and burned to the ground. News of the massacre spread east, further dampening future settlement in the northern reaches of the territory.

For four years, the charred ruins of Fort Dearborn remained untouched while war with the British raged along the Canadian border. The war ended in 1815, and a period of peace followed. Fort Dearborn

Below: **Flatboat used by early settlers**

was ordered rebuilt a year later on a larger scale and was more strongly garrisoned. After the war ended, the number of settlers did increase. Flatboats and barges carried emigrants down the Ohio River to Illinois. Other pioneers traveled by wagon across the Allegheny Mountains. Most newcomers, however, continued to settle in the wooded areas of southern Illinois while the vast, sparsely wooded prairies of central and northern Illinois remained largely uninhabited.

Shortly after Fort Dearborn was rebuilt, trade in northern Illinois also increased. One of the earliest traders was Gurdon Saltonstall Hubbard, whose influence on our area was to be considerable. Hubbard, a native of Vermont, was born in 1802. After moving with his family to Montreal, he became a trading post clerk with John Jacob Astor's American Fur Company in 1818. Later that year, Hubbard was assigned to the Illinois country, and he journeyed down the St. Lawrence River through the Great Lakes to the mouth of the Chicago River. Arriving in October at what was to become Chicago, Hubbard described the whitewashed buildings of Fort Dearborn and his first glimpses of Illinois prairie. The scene was so awe inspiring Hubbard later wrote he climbed a tree and gazed in admiration at the most beautiful site he had ever seen. "Waving green grass intermingled with a rich profusion of wild flowers . . . animated by a herd of deer and a pair of red foxes emerging from the grass within gunshot of me"—a wonderful sight to this industrious fur trader.

John Jacob Astor

In the mid-1820s, Hubbard established his own trading posts on the Iroquois River, a short distance from the present village of Watseka, and on the Vermillion River near the present site of Danville. To improve profits, Hubbard transported furs and trade goods between his trading posts and Chicago using pack ponies. Hubbard's pack trains followed an old Kickapoo Indian trail, originally tramped by migrating bison and elk on their way to ancient salt licks in southern Indiana and Kentucky. Hubbard's efforts met with great success, which led him to set up other posts about fifty miles apart south and west of Danville. His trade routes ultimately ended at Vincennes, Indiana.

Hubbard's Trace, as his trail was named, became an important link, bringing settlers and goods, between the more populated areas of southern Indiana and Illinois and the future metropolis of Chicago. The trail was later known as the Vincennes Trail and then the Chicago-

Vincennes Road. In 1834, parts of this trail were incorporated into the first state road designated Illinois Route 1. The trail initially traveled north to Chicago through Thornton in our area. In August 1853, a branch of the Chicago-Vincennes Road was opened north of what is now about Tenth Street in Chicago Heights, generally following the current path of the Dixie Highway through Homewood to Blue Island. Likely this branch was created to aid travelers in reaching the Illinois Central depot built on what became the west edge of downtown Homewood that same year.

Hubbard was a shrewd and prosperous businessman and had become one of Chicago's first leading citizens. Hubbard also gained fame as the "Paul Revere of the Prairies" when he dashed along his historic trail from Chicago to Danville to sound the alarm of a Winnebago uprising that threatened a second massacre at the Fort Dearborn post in 1827. Twenty hours after leaving Chicago, the intrepid Hubbard and his foaming horse reached Danville, a distance of about 150 miles. There he quickly organized a relief expedition to reinforce Fort Dearborn. With Hubbard in the lead, the "Vermillion Rangers" hurried northward, arriving in Chicago four days after Hubbard had left it. Shortly after their arrival, good news reached the fort that Chief Red Bird and his Winnebago warriors had already been captured.

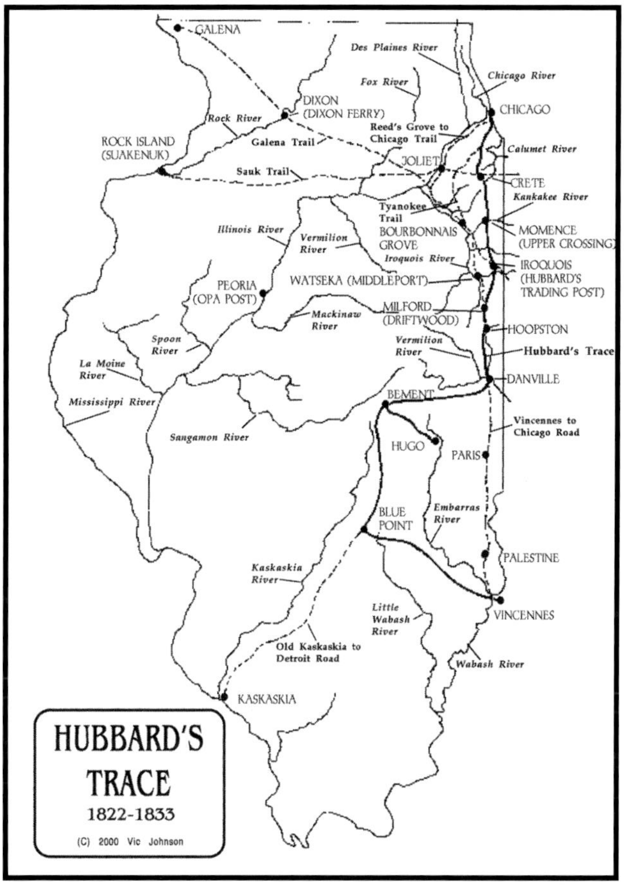

Map of Illinois and Hubbard's Trace *(Vic Johnson)*

Gurdon Saltonstall Hubbard *(Chicago Historical Society)*

The threat of Indian attacks like these became the single most important issue faced by settlers. At the time Illinois became a state in 1818, the non-Native American population was 35,000. Two years later, it increased to 55,000. More land was needed to accommodate this constant stream of settlers, which led to efforts to reduce the threats posed by the Indian population.

For years, the government had been making treaties with the Indians, acquiring more land from them for settlement by the westward bound. Discovery of lead in the hill country of northwestern Illinois hastened further conflict with the Indians as thousands of adventurous souls poured into the Indian lands of the upper Mississippi country near Galena to stake their claims. In 1830, seeking to make it safe for settlers moving into northern Illinois, the United States government required the Sauk and Fox to move to new lands west of the Mississippi in present-day Iowa. Once there, the tribes struggled to prepare the land for their crops, and many died from starvation during the brutal winter of 1831–32. In April 1832, Chief Black Hawk led about one thousand Sauk and Fox people back into northern Illinois to regain the ancestral farmland they had been forcibly removed from the year before. Fearing a revolt, settlers promptly organized a militia, which was augmented by federal troops. The military force included Abraham Lincoln, Jefferson Davis, and Zachary Taylor as young officers. Fierce battles ensued, and after just fifteen weeks of fighting, only about 150 of the Indian band survived, and Black Hawk surrendered on August 1, 1832.

Chief Black Hawk

The end of the Black Hawk War forever removed the "menace" of the Indian from Illinois lands east of the Mississippi. Word of this epoch event spread east, and shortly thereafter, the first wave of migration to northern Illinois from the northeastern and mid-Atlantic states, principally along the Erie Canal, completed in 1825, and east/west overland routes, like the Great Sauk Trail, began.

After the war, the Indians signed treaties ceding their remaining Illinois lands to the United States government. The land then became a part of the public domain to be surveyed and ultimately offered for sale to settlers. In our area, it was not until 1838 that the land was actually put up for public sale. By this time, many pioneers and their families had already homesteaded parcels: clearing the land, building cabins, and setting down roots. Acknowledging the efforts of these early homesteaders, who were essentially squatters, the U.S. Congress enacted "preemption" legislation, which allowed the settlers who could prove they had taken possession of their land before a specified date, the first opportunity to purchase the property they developed.

In northeastern Illinois, the government opened a district land office in Chicago in 1834 to handle all transactions in this part of the state. Initial sales of land in the area comprising what are now Thornton and Bloom Townships took place in 1838. Settlers here, who could prove they had taken possession of their land before February 22, 1838, were required to file an affidavit with the Chicago land office to that effect. Land office registrars then had the authority to accept or reject these "preemption" claims and, if accepted, affiants were allowed to purchase up to 160 acres at the bargain price of $1.25 per acre. Preemption landholders had to complete their transactions before the end of November 1838, after which, all unclaimed land could be sold to any buyer. These preemption claims give us an insight into who the first permanent settlers were.

Since Thornton and Bloom Townships were not officially organized until 1850, the townships were known on early surveys simply by their geographical coordinates. Township 35 north, range 14 east represented Bloom, and township 36 north, range 14 east represented Thornton. These numerical coordinates are still found on all local legal descriptions to this day.

In township 36 north (Thornton), Native American land claims in the Homewood area were denied, according to United States government land sales records researched by historian Margaret Kuch. The Treaty of Camp Tippecanoe of 1832 granted two sections of land "for the five daughters of Mo-nee, by her last husband, Joseph Bailly." Monee, an Indian "princess," was actually Marie LeFevre, a half-French, half-Ottawa Indian woman and daughter of a French fur trader. Her father died when she was eight, and her mother took her to live with Indian relatives. While called "Mah-ree" by the French, the Ottawa had no sound corresponding with the letter "r" and called Marie, "Mah-nee." French trading clerks later wrote the name as "Mo-nee."

Marie was married in 1810 to Joseph Bailly, a successful fur trader whose trading headquarters were located near present-day Chesterton, Indiana. The couple had five children, and Bailly, through his daughters' rights and at the demand of the Potawatomi, with whom his wife had much influence, bargained with U.S. land commissioners after the treaty ending the Black Hawk War was signed in October 1832. The five daughters of Monee claimed sections thirty-one and thirty-two of township 36 north, an area encompassing what is now Halsted Street to Western Avenue from 183rd to 175th Streets, but their claim for this land was denied in March 1837. The five daughters were subsequently granted 1,280 acres, two sections of land, centered around the intersection today known as Pauling Road and Egyptian Trail in the township now named for the "princess"—Monee.

Following the rejection of Native American interests in township 36 north (Thornton), Heman Crandall and Christopher Randall then filed preemption claims in the Homewood area. Crandall purchased the southeast quarter of section thirty-two, which is now north of 183rd Street and west of Halsted Street. Randall purchased the northwest quarter of section thirty-three, which is now south of 175th Street and east of Halsted Street. A quarter section comprised 160 acres.

In township 35 north (Bloom), a number of early settlers took advantage of the preemption law in the Homewood area. The most notable of these was Benjamin Butterfield. Butterfield, a native of Vermont, was born in 1795 and moved to Illinois in 1834. He purchased the southeast quarter of section six, which is the location of Idlewild Country Club today, farmed, and ran a "well-known tavern" there. Subsequently, Butterfield purchased land south of this parcel, and the creek that meandered through Butterfield's property has since been known by his name. Butterfield and his family moved from the area to Waterloo, Iowa, in the late 1850s, and he died there in 1878.

Benjamin Butterfield
(Flossmoor Public Library)

Across from Butterfield's land, Mehatabel Crary exercised her preemption rights and purchased the northwest quarter of section seven, now the southwest corner of the present intersection of Flossmoor Road and Dixie Highway and the land that encompasses a large part of the Flossmoor Country Club today. Farther east, James Barton bought the northwest quarter of section four, the land south of 183rd and east of Halsted Streets. David Crandall, Heman's brother, purchased the adjoining acreage, the northeast quarter of section five, now south of 183rd Street and west of Halsted Street. Early sources place the Crandalls in Illinois before 1832, the year the family had to retreat to the shelter of Fort Dearborn during the Black Hawk War.

After these preemption claims were satisfied, the first public land sale for other parcels in these townships took place in Chicago on

November 29, 1838. Land speculators and agents representing them purchased large sections of these and adjoining townships. The names of Thomas Dyer, Julius Wadsworth, Sylvester Bowen, and later John Lewis appear frequently as purchasers and then as sellers, lending credence to the speculative nature of their transactions. William Storm, William Young, and John and Job Campbell were those in the Homewood area who completed post-preemption purchases of land before the close of 1838.

Through the 1840s, other settlers from the east homesteaded in the area that was to become known as Homewood. Near Benjamin Butterfield's place, Edwin Bump and his family, which grew to include ten children, settled on forty acres near the present-day intersection of Holbrook Road and Dixie Highway. A short distance to the north, brothers Cyrus and Cornelius Eastwood purchased and farmed forty acres apiece across the Vincennes Road from one another. Cyrus Eastwood's property was the northwest corner of what is now Dixie Highway and Flossmoor Road, while Cornelius owned the land at the northeast corner of 187th Street and Dixie Highway.

Continuing north, George Morris and his family moved to our area from Pennsylvania in the mid-1840s and initially settled on eighty acres west of the Vincennes Road (Dixie Highway) between what is now Willow Road and 187th Street. In 1849, a short distance from the Morris farm, Horace Briggs, his wife Sarah, and six children settled on the acreage that encompasses most of Ravisloe Country Club today.

A mile east of the Briggs farm and west of the current intersection of Ridge Road and Center Avenue, David Hood settled on 160 acres that extended farther west to what is now Ashland Avenue and included the area now north of 183rd Street. East of Hood's farm, Samuel and Ann James purchased the quarter section in 1848 that Heman Crandall had homesteaded just a decade before. The James farm also covered the area a half-mile north of what is now 183rd Street, from Halsted Street west to Center Avenue.

Sam James was not a farmer by trade and actually worked for years at the Ryerson Steel Company in Chicago. To help manage the family farm, James convinced Robert Gillespie, a good friend from Ireland, to

Samuel James
(Jean Mackenzie)

Left: **Ann James**
(Jean Mackenzie)

The James home was located on land now south of Ridge Road east of Center Avenue. ***(Jean Mackenzie)***

Below: **Robert Gillespie** ***(Jean Mackenzie)***

immigrate to the United States. Gillespie was a good farmer and also made a name for himself raising thoroughbred horses. He was active in the community and was an early member of the First Presbyterian Church. The James family initially occupied a cabin Heman Crandall had built on the north side of the road that led to the Thornton settlement (Ridge Road). A few years later, the family built a frame house on the south side of the road. Sam James died in 1878, and, in 1879, Ann took in her motherless one-year-old niece, Margaret Black, to live with her. Ann died in 1906, and the farm was deeded to Margaret a few years later. In 1910, Margaret married Alick Mackenzie, a Scotsman who was a merchant marine engineer, not a farmer. Hired men did the farm work, and the family built a much larger home in 1916 that still stands at 1055 Ridge Road. Donald Mackenzie, the last member of the James and Mackenzie families to occupy the home, moved away in 1980, over 130 years after the family first settled on the land.

Northwest of the James farm, James Hart and his family settled on 160 acres in the southwest quarter of section twenty-nine of Thornton Township sometime between 1846–1849. Hart's farm was located on land that is now north and east of the corner of 175th Street and Ashland Avenue. For years it was believed that Hart and his family were the first settlers in Homewood, arriving sometime in 1834. Extensive research by historian Margaret Kuch debunked this long-held notion.

Her research of land and census records revealed that Hart was born in about 1820, probably in Wayne County, Indiana. On October 18, 1840, James married Sally Ann Wright while still living in Wayne County. The 1850 census indicated Hart's four-year-old daughter Rebecca was born in Indiana, while his one-year-old son Henry was born in Illinois, further narrowing down the dates the family immigrated to Illinois. Regardless of when Hart arrived in the area, he alone would have a significant impact on the location of downtown Homewood, and he would also be instrumental in seeing to it that the educational needs of the children of the area were met.

Conrad Hecht and family posing in front of their home which still stands at 18916 Dixie Highway.

By the mid-1840s, the first of what was to become a steady stream of German immigrants arrived in the Homewood area. In 1846, Liborius Hupe, his wife Anna, and their five children settled on one hundred acres in the northeast quarter of section thirty-six in Bremen Township, land now south of 175th Street and west of Western Avenue. In 1849, Conrad Hecht purchased land formerly owned by Cyrus Eastwood in section six of Bloom Township.

By 1861, Hecht owned two hundred acres in sections six and seven in that township, including the land Mehatabel Crary purchased under the preemption act in 1838. Hecht later sold this land to the organizers of the Flossmoor Country Club in 1899, and much of the remaining acreage surrounding his homestead was sold to the developers of the Flossmoor Park subdivision in 1925. The Hecht family farmhouse, a well-preserved example of our area's earliest architecture, is still standing at 18916 Dixie Highway, just south of Homewood's current village limits.

Left: Samuel Riegel *(Meyer Estate)*

Another family who came from Germany to the area during the 1840s was the Samuel Riegel family. Riegel immigrated to the United States with his second wife Ottilia and his nine children. Samuel's first wife,

Top right:
George Riegel
(Meyer Estate)

Bottom right:
Friedaricka Riegel
(Meyer Estate)

Facing page:
George and Friedaricka Riegel's children stand next to the family home which stood on the east side of Riegel Road just north of what is now 187th Street.
(Meyer Estate)

Facing page, inset:
Sons Edward (l) and Adolph (r) sit beside their father George Riegel behind the family farmhouse on Riegel Road.
(Meyer Estate)

Anna Margaretha, mother of seven of the children, had died in 1842.

The Riegels initially settled in Chicago and had moved to southern Cook County in the early 1850s. Samuel owned land in Bremen Township northwest of Cooper's Grove, present-day Country Club Hills, and he also owned a forty-acre parcel in section five of Bloom Township bounded by what today is Willow Road on the north, 187th Street on the south, Ashland Avenue on the west, and Loomis Avenue on the east. By the time of the 1860 federal census, Riegel's oldest son George was farming this parcel and living there with his sister Margaret and brother Michael. Samuel Riegel continued to live on his Cooper's Grove farm until about 1865 when he and his wife moved in with his son George, George's wife Friedaricka, and their growing family.

George Riegel had been sickly as a youth, and it was because of this the family moved from Chicago. Fresh air, farming, and country living must have agreed with George as he lived to the ripe old age of ninety-four and fathered ten children, five boys and five girls. Shortly after George Riegel's death in 1926, the family farm on the road that bears his name was sold to developers. The onset of the Depression, however, saw to it that the residential development planned for the property was delayed. Home building on the Riegel farm would not take place until the 1960s, well over thirty years later.

These are the names of many of the first settlers in Homewood. Most of the Germans stayed and built new lives for themselves and their families. Many of the "Yankees" heeded the call of Horace Greeley and moved west, selling their farms here, reaping profits, and buying more acreage in western states at lower prices.

Scene from an early settler's wagon trip west to Illinois

CHAPTER 2
The Railroad Arrives

By 1850, settlers continued to migrate into the state of Illinois at a steady rate. Most, however, were still concentrating near rivers, navigable creeks, and other bodies of water that assured them good transportation routes. Ground transportation was often unreliable. Wagon trails were nothing more than rutted paths, which were passable in good weather but quickly became impassable in wet weather. All too frequently, wagon wheels sank to their hubs on rain-choked trails and became hopelessly bogged in the mire. Aid had to be sought from nearby farms, if there were any, to help extricate the stranded rigs. Journeys that normally would have taken a day or two over dry land were doubled or even tripled in time in poor weather.

With such poor transportation conditions to contend with, the fertile prairies surrounding Homewood and found in much of the state remained sparsely settled despite the fact the federal government had over eleven million acres of land for sale at a price of a mere $1.25 per acre.

For years, state legislators had considered the proposition of a "central" railroad, which would run the length of the state. This railroad would provide reliable transportation for farm products and other goods and would serve as an impetus to settling the vast stretches of open land throughout the state.

In 1837, the Illinois State Legislature passed the Internal Improvement Act, calling for more than thirteen hundred miles of state-owned railroads extending into all parts of Illinois, except the northeast corner, which they felt would be best served by the Illinois and Michigan Canal, begun a year earlier. This massive rail project was to be financed by borrowing an estimated $10 million. Like many government undertakings, this amount was soon determined to be less than half enough. The state government found itself committed to a debt of $20 million, and by 1840, the rail project collapsed, leaving the state with a huge debt burden and, remarkably, with only twenty-four miles of completed railroad.

During the ensuing decade, Illinois citizens had little taste for any new rail projects. By 1850, their appetites improved somewhat, and a forty-two-mile stretch of railroad was completed between Chicago and Elgin with a ten-mile branch connecting with Aurora. This line was known as the Galena and Chicago Union (predecessor of the Chicago Northwestern), its name indicating the ultimate west and east termini of the route.

Also that year, Illinois' two United States senators, Sidney A. Breese and Stephen A. Douglas, introduced separate legislation for a grant of federal public lands to aid in the construction of the long-abandoned central railroad plan. After much debate, the bill submitted by Douglas passed both houses of Congress and was signed into law by President Millard Fillmore on September 20, 1850. The bill provided for the transfer of 2,595,000 acres of public lands to the state of Illinois for the purpose of building a railroad that would speed the opening of the inaccessible prairies of the interior of the state, speed the sale of and increase the value of the remaining federal lands, and would ultimately increase the amount of federal taxes collected in the state.

Above: **Senator Sidney A. Breese**

Right: **Senator Stephen A. Douglas**

Given its past track record, the state sought private investment groups to carry out the construction of the railroad. On February 10, 1851, the Illinois State Legislature granted a charter to a group headed by Robert Rantoul of Massachusetts for the Illinois Central Railroad Company. The charter granted the company all of the 2,595,000 acres of public land previously transferred to the state and set forth numerous conditions, chief of which were the railroad should be completed within six years and the company should pay the state seven cents on every dollar received from freight and passenger traffic.

With this, the railroad company set about formulating plans for the construction of 705 miles of track that would stretch from Cairo in the south to Galena in the northwest and include a branch to Chicago in the northeast portion of the state. Galena, a prosperous mining town, was considered the more important of the northern towns, and the "main line" of the railroad was initially routed there. It was not long, however, before the 366-mile stretch from Cairo to Chicago was bustling with traffic and became the true "main line" of the road.

Robert Rantoul, leader of the group granted a charter to form the Illinois Central Railroad

Since one of the main purposes of the Illinois Central Railroad was to "settle the prairies," the route selected to Chicago did not pass through a single settlement of more than one hundred inhabitants and only passed near three of any importance—Bourbonnais on the Kankakee River with 1,710 inhabitants; Urbana in central Illinois with 210 inhabitants; and, in our area, Thornton with about 150 inhabitants, three miles east of where the track was finally laid. The rest of the land was largely uninhabited and "a place where one could travel a whole day without seeing another person."

Construction of the railroad commenced on December 23, 1851, and ground was broken at both Cairo and Chicago. The job was laborious to say the least. Almost everything had to be done by hand using picks, shovels, and sledgehammers. Thousands of men were recruited from east coast cities, Ireland, Germany, and other countries to provide the labor needed. It was estimated there were up to ten thousand men at times working up and down the rails on this project. Raw materials had to come from distant places. Lumber came from the forests of the north woods and southern Illinois, iron rails were purchased in England and were shipped by boat and barge to the prairies, stone came from the quarries in and around Illinois, and food came from far and near to feed the voracious appetites of the laborers.

Early Homewood settler Ann James would often tell of the day railroad surveyors came to her door asking if she could prepare a dinner for them. As she and her family had just completed their noon meal, she obliged and sent the men out to gather wood chips for her fire. On their return, a fine meal was ready, and the men were well satisfied. When the men had finished eating, they asked how much they owed her for their dinners. Mrs. James replied nothing at all as she was happy to accommodate them. To her surprise, she found a silver dollar under

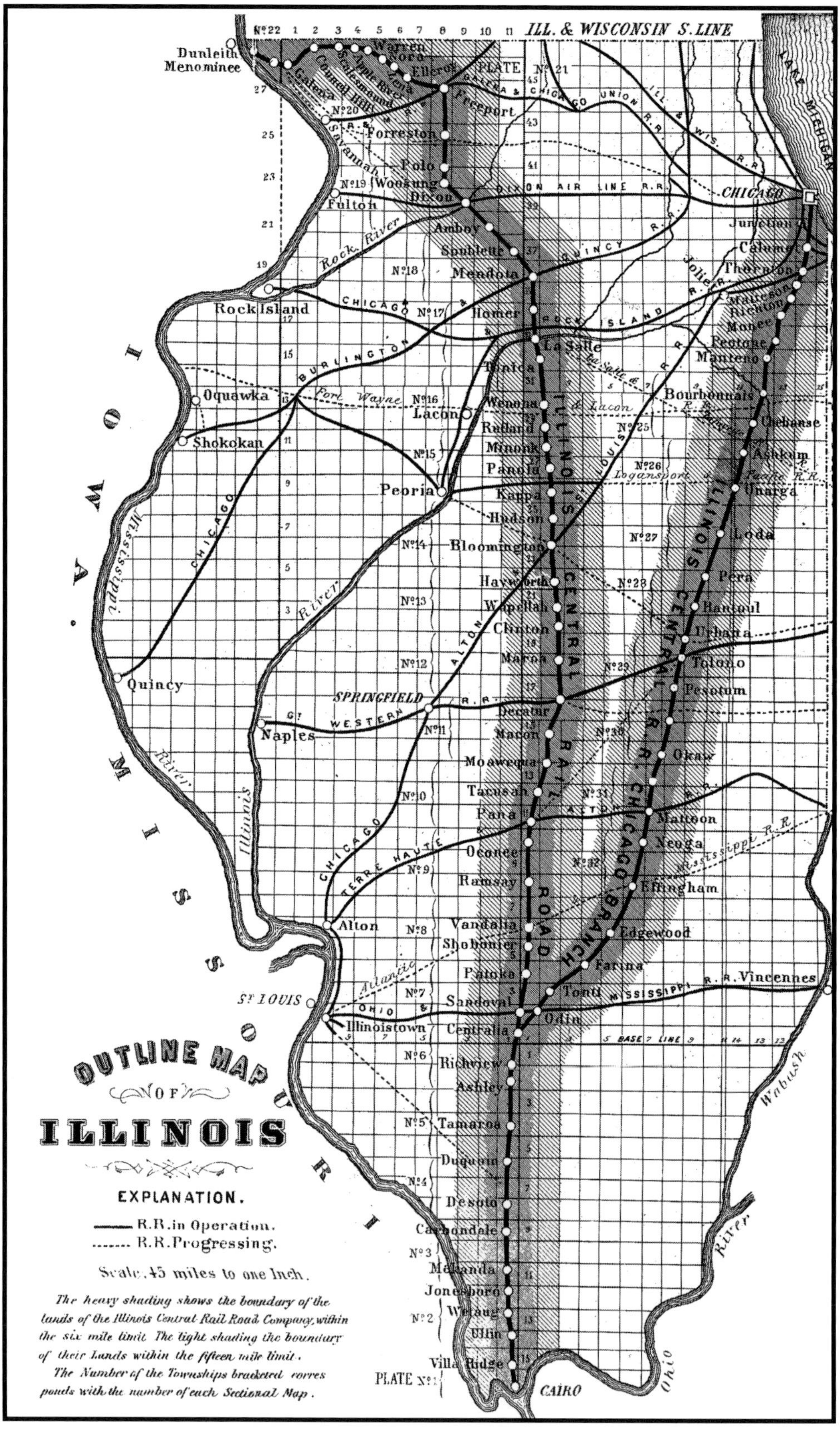
ILL. & WISCONSIN S. LINE
LAKE MICHIGAN
CHICAGO
IOWA
MISSOURI
Mississippi River
Illinois River
Rock River
Wabash River
Ohio River
ILLINOIS CENTRAL RAIL ROAD
ILLINOIS CENTRAL R.R. CHICAGO BRANCH
SPRINGFIELD
ST LOUIS
CAIRO
Dunleith
Menominee
Galena
Freeport
Dixon
Mendota
La Salle
Peoria
Bloomington
Decatur
Mattoon
Effingham
Centralia
Carbondale
Rock Island
Quincy
Alton
Vincennes
PLATE No 21
PLATE No 1
OUTLINE MAP
OF
ILLINOIS
EXPLANATION.
R.R. in Operation.
R.R. Progressing.
Scale 45 miles to one Inch.
The heavy shading shows the boundary of the lands of the Illinois Central Rail Road Company, within the six mile limit. The light shading the boundary of their Lands within the fifteen mile limit.
The Number of the Townships bracketed corresponds with the number of each Sectional Map.

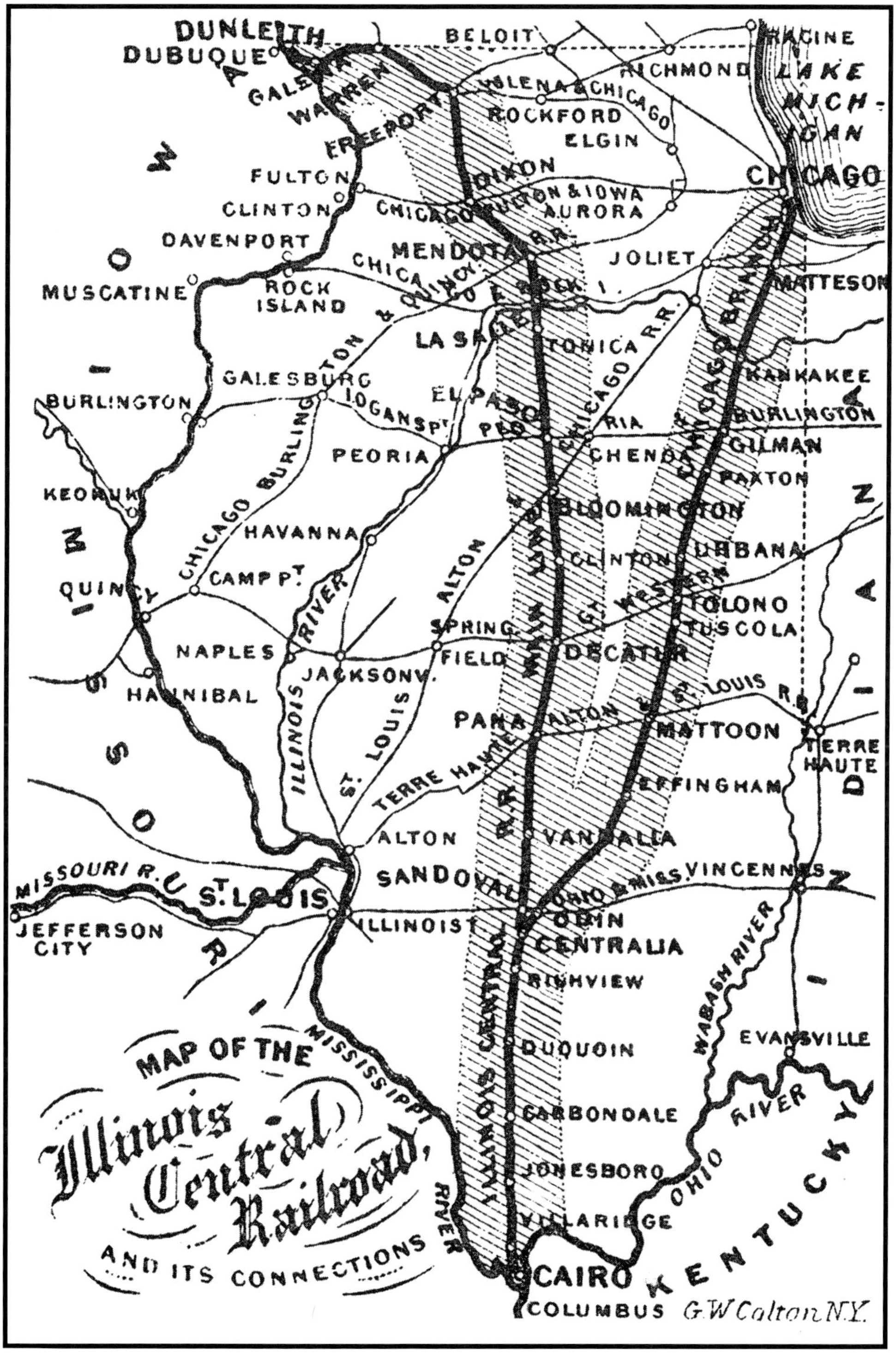

Maps showing the original routes of the Illinois Central Railroad

Railroad workers lay track on the wide-open prairies.

Right: Illinois Central advertisement recruits laborers to help build the railroad.

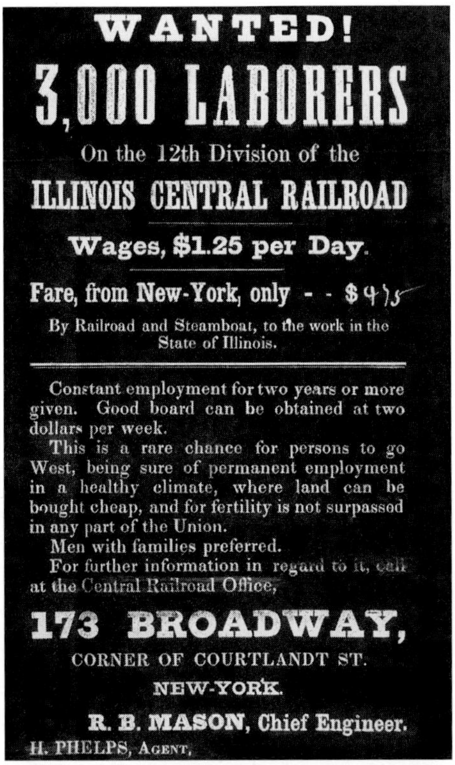

each of their plates while clearing the table after the men had left. A fine payment for such a good deed!

Despite logistical problems and other hardships, construction on the railroad proceeded at a breakneck pace. On May 20, 1852, the first portion of the railroad completed between Chicago and Calumet (Kensington) was opened for traffic. Work proceeded south, and on July 11, 1853, a crew train arrived from Chicago at Kankakee to signal completion of the line to that settlement. The first passenger excursion train from Chicago to Kankakee, which stopped at what is now present-day Homewood, took place on August 5, 1853.

The coming of the "iron horse" was undoubtedly the most important factor in the growth and development of Homewood. Homewood, however, was not the first name given by the railroad to the depot they built on the east side of the track just south of the Thornton Road

(Ridge Road). When Illinois Central engineers surveyed the area in 1851, they reported only a few houses visible from the point selected to establish the station. Since the depot was meant to serve Thornton, the thriving settlement to the east, the surveyors dubbed the spot "Thornton Station." The name soon found its way onto railroad maps and would identify the stop for almost two decades.

The arrival of the Illinois Central's engine number 1 signaled the opening of the railroad in towns up and down the line in 1853.

The railroad's depot was completed in 1853 and was a utilitarian one-and-one-half-story wood frame structure that included living quarters on the second floor for the station agent and his family. George Churchill was the first station agent appointed by the railroad, and he also served as the first postmaster for Thornton Station.

The rail stop, like a highway interchange today, served as a magnet for development. James Hart, seeing this potential, purchased, in

Homewood's first rail depot was located on the east side of the tracks, just south of what is now Ridge Road. The depot was built in 1853.

1852, the land that would become the central part of Homewood's future business district. A plat of survey subdividing this land under the name "Hartford" was filed with the Cook County Recorder in 1853. Hart later sold lots for business and residential use, and his desire was for the settlement that was beginning to grow around the rail stop to be officially known as Hartford. Despite his desires, the predominance of the railroad won out, and the name Thornton Station endured.

The first commercial buildings erected in what was to become downtown Homewood were built in 1853 on what is now the southeast corner of Ridge Road and Harwood Avenue.

Hart's speculation did prove fruitful. Development soon followed. Henry Brinkman purchased a lot and built a hotel and saloon on the north side of the Thornton Road several lots east of the railroad right-of-way in 1852. Thornton Road, an old Indian trail, was later known as Main Street and is now known as Ridge Road. Most of the early development took place on this street west of the Chicago-Vincennes Road (Dixie Highway).

In 1853, Charles Robinson, a prominent Blue Island merchant, purchased several lots and built a general store with hotel rooms above it on the south side of Thornton Road directly east of the rail depot. Louis Oswald took charge of the store, which was later operated by Thomas Hastings, while Robinson managed affairs from his shop in Blue Island. Also that year, another Robinson, Alfred by name and who was of no relation to Charles, opened another general store on the north side of Thornton Road several lots east of the Brinkman Hotel.

The settlement continued to grow and by 1855 had a population of 120 inhabitants. The Illinois Central annual report of 1855 described Thornton Station as a " small place but the land surrounding the station is well cultivated with large corn and wheat fields and at least 30 farm houses and farms are in sight of the depot." This was certainly quite a difference from the description given by surveyors four years earlier.

The trade of local residents, along with travelers frequenting the rail depot, supported the opening of a third general store established by brothers Henry and Conrad Zimmer in 1855. Henry had clerked in C. D. Robinson's store in Blue Island before coming to Thornton Station. He set up his own shop in a small house rented from Henry Brinkman, which was located between the Brinkman Hotel and Alfred Robinson's store on the north side of Thornton Road. A year later, a new building was built next door to house their general store. After this, Henry Zimmer took over sole operation of the business. Henry was to become active in community affairs over the next decades. He was appointed to serve several stints as postmaster of the community and served in this capacity for a total of thirty years. During this period, he would pick up the day's mail at the depot and then distribute it to residents at his store. This increased traffic in his store, which must have certainly helped to boost his bottom line. He was elected to serve various terms as Thornton Township clerk, justice of the peace, and collector of taxes. Zimmer was also involved in religious affairs and was one of the individuals who helped to organize St. Paul Church.

The increased cultivation of the former prairies surrounding Thornton Station also led to the establishment of one of its largest businesses—a steam-flouring mill. The mill was built in 1856 adjacent to the railroad track about two blocks south of the depot. The foundation walls still stand and have been incorporated as part of the building that is located at 18216 Harwood Avenue. Area farmers contributed funds for construction of the mill on a "subscription" basis. Depending on

Henry Zimmer's store was built on the north side of Main Street (Ridge Road) east of the railroad tracks in the mid-1850s.

Thornton Station's steam flour mill was built in 1856. The mill was later purchased by August Steiner. The foundation walls still exist as part of the building at 18216 Harwood Avenue.

the amount contributed, a farmer was given shares in the company that was formed to operate the mill. George W. Morris was elected president of the company, and the mill was a success from the start. Other mills in the area were wind powered and depended on the whims of the weather to operate. Many a farmer would drive a wagonload of grain to one of these mills only to find the wind had died down by the time he arrived, preventing his grain from being ground promptly. Thornton Station's steam-operated mill had no such problem; it operated on windy days and calm ones. Farmers were soon coming from long distances, bypassing other mills, to have their grain dependably ground at Thornton Station. The increased business at the mill meant increased patronage for other Thornton Station businesses. Farmers would stop for a cold beer and hot lunch at the saloon or to purchase hardware, staple goods, and other sundries at the general stores.

Morris also saw the potential for further development in Thornton Station and purchased forty acres located east of the mill and adjoining the Hart subdivision on the south. This acreage was laid out in residential lots and subdivided under the name "Thornton Station" in 1856. Sales of lots were brisk for a time, but the economic Panic of 1857 discouraged further speculation in "suburban" real estate for a number of years to come.

With the continued growth of Thornton Station, residents began to attend to the educational and spiritual needs of the community. James Hart was instrumental in establishing a public school. He deeded some of his land to the school trustees of Thornton Township, and this transfer was recorded in 1855. Shortly thereafter, a one-room schoolhouse was constructed on this property, which was located east of the railroad track and near the present-day intersection of Dixie Highway and Harwood Avenue, where the old Homewood Library building now stands. Hart, who farmed 160 acres located at the northeast corner of the present-day intersection of 175th Street and Ashland Avenue, no doubt wanted the school located as close as possible to his home to cut down on the distances his children would have to walk daily to and from school.

By 1858, early settlers had also grown tired of the lack of any permanent religious organization in the community. Occasionally, an itinerant preacher or circuit rider would stop and hold services in the home of a local resident, but the people of Thornton Station yearned for a church and preacher of their own. Although the decade of the 1850s saw a large influx of German settlers, the original settlers were primarily of English and Scotch-Irish descent from New England and other eastern states. Many had attended Presbyterian churches near their former homes, and this denomination was the first to establish a church at Thornton Station. An organizational meeting was held on December 19, 1858, under the direction of Rev. A. W. Henderson. At this meeting, ten members of the community, including three from the Caldwell family and four from the Morehead family, "gave their public assent to the articles of faith and entered into covenant with each other

The original First Presbyterian Church was located on the east side of the Illinois Central tracks just north of what is now the Dixie Highway viaduct.

as a church." The First Presbyterian Church of Thornton Station was now a reality. Within weeks, seven new members were added to the rolls, including David and Mary Hood. Early church services were held in the public schoolhouse, and fundraising was started immediately for a proper building. Construction commenced within months on a church, and this building was located north of the schoolhouse and east of the railroad right-of-way.

With homes, businesses, a school, and a church, Thornton Station lacked only one thing to ensure the continued health and growth of

Dr. William Doepp and his wife Pauline ***(Doris Waldschmidt)***

The Doepp's first home was located adjacent to Butterfield Creek near what is now Western Avenue north of Vollmer Road. ***(Doris Waldschmidt)***

The Doepp family home was built in 1872 on the Chicago-Vincennes Road (Dixie Highway) in Homewood.

the community—a doctor. This situation was soon remedied when twenty-seven-year-old physician William Doepp, a German immigrant, settled along Butterfield Creek near what is now Vollmer Road and Western Avenue in 1859. Doepp moved to this area with his young bride, Pauline, and her obituary in 1928 chronicled the hardships they faced.

"The young pioneer couple had just been married at the little frontier outpost called Milwaukee and they came down to Illinois to help in the development of the Great Plains. Wild forests rose on all sides of the old farmhouse near Butterfield Creek and still wilder animals roamed at large over the plains and among the trees and brush."

"Young Dr. Doepp started to engage actively in the practice of medicine and was the first physician to practice in this territory. He rode through blizzards of snow and sleet, hundreds of miles, sometimes, in a single week on his errands of mercy. At times he was gone for days, would return to his home, rest a few hours and then set out to bring health to some unfortunate person on the Great Plains—some fellow pioneer." It was said in these early years Doepp would visit patients in an area that extended as far east as Crown Point and as far west as New Lenox.

The Illinois Central, in later years, allowed trains to stop near the Doepp farm so patients could disembark and visit his office. The stop was called the "doctor's crossing," and this considerably reduced the amount of travel Doepp had to make to complete his rounds.

In 1872, Doepp and his family moved to Thornton Station to a home built on the Chicago-Vincennes Road (Dixie Highway) across from St. Paul Church. The home had a large greenhouse attached to it and was situated on well-manicured grounds that included a sledding hill and a large pond that generations of children enjoyed swimming in during the summer and skating on in the winter. The family loved animals and, in addition to dogs and horses, more exotic species such as deer, peacocks, a monkey, and two Mexican ant bears named Chico and Jane graced their estate at one time.

The Doepps were blessed with ten children, six boys and four girls. Three of Dr. Doepp's sons, William, Edward and Frederick, would follow in his footsteps and become physicians themselves, while son Albert became a dentist. The youngest son, Herman, was a lifesaver of a different sort. An engineer, he worked on a Mexican sugar cane plan-

Some young bathers enjoy a refreshing "dip" in Doepp's Pond. Note the bathing suits and caps these young ladies are wearing.

tation and died while trying to save a colleague who had become asphyxiated by fumes in a vat of cane juice. Coworkers had pulled Herman to safety after his initial rescue attempt failed. Undaunted, Herman reentered the vat a second time and, tragically, succumbed to the fumes himself.

Dr. Doepp was very active in political affairs and was elected to serve as Thornton Township supervisor. He was appointed as Homewood's first village treasurer and was elected to serve as Homewood's second village president in 1896. Sons Frederick and Albert would also follow their father into politics, and each served terms as Homewood village president. Dr. Doepp died suddenly in April 1897, after a bout with pneumonia, at the height of his political and professional career.

As the decade of the 1850s drew to a close, the rapid transformation of the land surrounding Thornton Station, due in large part to the railroad, was readily apparent. In ten short years, the area had gone from one of largely unsettled prairies to one of well-cultivated farm fields anchored by a growing town.

Top left:* Pauline Doepp in later years *(Doris Waldschmidt)

Left:* Dr. William Doepp, Homewood's first village treasurer and second village president *(Village of Homewood)

Below left:* Dr. Frederick Doepp, Homewood village president from 1898–1900 *(Doris Waldschmidt)

Below:* Dr. Albert Doepp, Homewood village president from 1901–1906 *(Village of Homewood)

Farm on the prairies of Illinois

Homes for the Industrious!

IN THE

GARDEN STATE OF THE WEST.

THE ILLINOIS CENTRAL RAILROAD CO., HAVE FOR SALE

1,200,000 ACRES OF RICH FARMING LANDS,

In Tracts of Forty Acres and upward, on Long Credit and at Low Prices.

MECHANICS, FARMERS AND WORKING MEN.

THE attention of the enterprising and industrious portion of the community is directed to the following statements and liberal inducements offered them by the

ILLINOIS CENTRAL RAILROAD COMPANY.

which, as they will perceive, will enable them by proper energy, perseverance and industry, to provide comfortable homes for themselves and families, with, comparatively speaking, very little capital.

LANDS OF ILLINOIS.

No State in the Valley of the Mississippi offers so great an inducement as the State of Illinois. There is no portion of the world where all the conditions of climate and soil so admirably combine to produce those two great staples, CORN and WHEAT, as the Prairies of Illinois.

THE SOUTHERN PART

of the State lies within the zone of the cotton regions, while the soil is admirably adapted to the growth of tobacco and hemp; and the wheat is worth from fifteen to twenty cents more per bushel than that raised further north.

RICH ROLLING PRAIRIE LANDS.

The deep rich loam of the prairies is cultivated with such wonderful facility that the farmers of the Eastern and Middle States are moving to Illinois in great numbers. The area of Illinois is about equal to that of England, and the soil is so rich that it will support twenty millions of people.

EASTERN AND SOUTHERN MARKETS.

These lands are contiguous to a railroad 700 miles in length, which connects with other roads and navigable lakes and rivers, thus affording an unbroken communication with the Eastern and Southern markets.

APPLICATION OF CAPITAL.

Thus far, capital and labor have been applied to developing the soil; the great resources of the State in coal and iron are almost untouched. The invariable rule that the mechanical arts flourish best where food and fuel are cheapest, will follow at an early day in Illinois, and in the course of the next ten years the natural laws and necessities of the case warrant the belief that at least five hundred thousand people will be engaged in the State of Illinois in various manufacturing pursuits.

RAILROAD SYSTEM OF ILLINOIS.

Over $100,000,000 of private capital have been expended on the railways of Illinois. Inasmuch as part of the income from several these works, with a valuable public fund in lands, go to diminish the State expenses, the TAXES ARE LIGHT, and must consequently every day decrease.

THE STATE DEBT.

The State Debt is only $10,105,398, 14, and within the last three years has been reduced $2,959,746 80, and we may reasonably expect that in ten years it will become extinct.

PRESENT POPULATION.

The State is rapidly filling up with population; 868,025 persons having been added since 1850, making the present population 1,723,663, a ratio of 102 per cent. in ten years.

AGRICULTURAL PRODUCTS.

The Agricultural products of Illinois are greater than those of any other State. The products sent out during the past year exceeded 1,500,000 tons. The wheat crop of 1860 approaches 35,000,000 bushels, while the corn crop yields not less than 140,000,000 bushels.

FERTILITY OF THE SOIL.

Nowhere can the industrious farmer secure such immediate results for his labor as upon these prairie soils, they being composed of a deep rich loam, the fertility of which, is unsurpassed by any on the globe.

TO ACTUAL CULTIVATORS.

Since 1854, the company have sold 1,300,000 acres. They sell only to actual cultivators, and every contract co tains an agreement to cultivate. The road has been const ucted thro' these lands at an expense of $30,000,000. In 1850 the population of the forty-nine counties through which it passes was only 335,598; since which 479,293 have been added, making the whole population 814,891, a gain of 143 per cent.

EVIDENCES OF PROSPERITY.

As an evidence of the thrift of the people, it may be stated that 600,000 tons of freight, including 8,600,000 bushels of grain, and 250,000 barrels of flour, were forwarded over the line last year.

EDUCATION.

Mechanics and workingmen will find the free school system encouraged by the State, and endowed with a large revenue for the support of schools. Their children can live in sight of the church and schoolhouse and grow with the prosperity of the leading State in the Great Western Empire.

PRICES AND TERMS OF PAYMENT.

The prices of these lands vary from $6 to $25 per acre according to location, quality, &c. First-class farming lands sell for about $10 or $12 per acre; and the relative expense of subduing prairie land as compared with wood lands is in the ratio of 1 to 10 in favor of the former. The terms of sale for the bulk of these lands will be

One Year's Interest in advance,

at six per ct. per annum, and six interest notes at six per ct. payable respectively in one, two, three, four, five and six years from date of sale; and four notes for principal, payable in four, five, six and seven years from date of sale; the contract stipulating that one-tenth of the tract purchased shall be fenced and cultivated, each and every year, for five years from date of sale, so that at the end of five years, one-half shall be fenced and under cultivation.

Twenty Per Cent. will be deducted

from the valuation for cash, except the same should be at six dollars per acre, when the cash price will be five dollars.

Pamphlets descriptive of the lands, soil, climate, productions, prices and terms of payment, can be had on application to

J. W. FOSTER, Land Commissioner, Chicago, Illinois.

For the names of the Towns, Villages and Cities situated upon the Illinois Central Railroad see pages 188, 189, 190, APPLETON'S RAILWAY GUIDE.

Illinois Central Railroad advertisement extolling the virtues of Illinois

CHAPTER 3
The Civil War Years

As residents of the state of Illinois ushered in the year 1860, they too realized the impact the Illinois Central Railroad had on the growth of the state. In 1850, Illinois had a population of 851,470 while by 1860, the population had more than doubled to 1,711,951. The railroad had lived up to its promise of opening the prairies to settlement. Nowhere was this growth more apparent than in Thornton Station and the townships that surrounded it. By 1860, Thornton Station had grown to a population of 260. The following chart shows the growth in the adjacent townships.

Township	1850	1860
Thornton	369	1,033
Bloom	785	1,228
Bremen	250	790
Rich	168	1,143

The Illinois Central Railroad actively promoted the state. Advertisements were placed in newspapers in eastern cities and foreign countries. In addition, hundreds of thousands of pamphlets touting the advantages of Illinois were distributed to prospective settlers in the east and to immigrants arriving at U.S. seaports. The growth that began in the 1850s was sure to continue in the 1860s. The future of the state looked bright. Troubling times, however, were on the horizon.

For years, the nation had struggled with the question of slavery. The South's economy was driven by agriculture, and cotton, its chief crop, represented 57 percent of all U.S. exports. In order to maintain a level of profitability, southern plantation owners were dependent on slavery as the essential component of their labor supply. The North, in contrast, was firmly established as an industrial society. Large numbers of skilled and semi-skilled laborers, not slaves, were needed to work in their factories. The North encouraged immigration from other countries, and very few immigrants settled in the South.

To further complicate matters, the North's economy needed networks of turnpikes, canals, and railroads to move its goods to market. The federal government built much of this infrastructure, and its chief source of revenue was tariffs on imported goods. The North demanded high tariffs not only to support these improvements but also to protect their manufactured goods from foreign imports. The South, conversely, had little need for elaborate transportation systems, and as it manufactured little, most products were imported. Southerners opposed high tariffs, which increased the price on goods they imported and threatened the volume of cotton they exported.

President Abraham Lincoln

For most of the 1800s, Congress tried to maintain a delicate balance between the interests of the North and South—the non-slave and the slave states. In 1819, the United States Senate was perfectly balanced between these interests, but that balance did not last long. For the next four decades, Congress crafted a series of laws—the Missouri Compromise, the Compromise of 1850, and the Kansas-Nebraska Act—to attempt to reconcile the divergent interests of the North and South. By 1860, this task had become almost impossible, and with the election of Abraham Lincoln to the presidency that year, the South had had enough. Lincoln had argued slavery was "a moral, a social and a political wrong," and many in the South feared Lincoln would threaten that institution.

Confederate General P. G. T. Beauregard

Before Lincoln was even sworn into office in March 1861, seven southern states had seceded from the Union and formed the Confederate States of America. This conflict reached the boiling point on April 12, 1861, when Confederate General P. G. T. Beauregard and his troops opened fire on Fort Sumter in Charleston Harbor, igniting the start of the Civil War.

To quell the Confederate rebellion, President Lincoln issued a proclamation calling for troops from each of the states that remained in the Union. At this time, little could anyone imagine the war would last four long years and claim over 600,000 lives.

Young men from the area in and around Thornton Station responded to the Union's call for help. During the first two years of the war, many voluntarily enlisted for service. By 1863, the Union had initiated a draft, and in July 1864, registration rolls listed 225 men in Thornton Township, 198 in Bremen Township, 140 in Bloom Township, and 149 in Rich Township available for duty if needed. War records in the Illinois State Archives indicate about twenty men entered active service from Thornton Station and the area immediately surrounding it.

John Caldwell, John George Riegel, and William Seymour mustered into service with the Thirty-ninth Illinois Infantry, which was organized shortly after the assault on Fort Sumter but not accepted into federal service until after the disastrous first battle at Bull Run. The Thirty-ninth saw hard fighting in Virginia and also witnessed the final surrender of Lee at Appomattox.

September 1861 saw a number of Illinois units mustered into federal service with men from Thornton Station. Richard Caldwell and Benjamin Morris were assigned to the Eighth Illinois Cavalry, which would engage the Confederates in battle at Antietam, Manassas, and Gettysburg. Marcellus E. Jones, a lieutenant in the Eighth Illinois from DuPage County, is reputed to have fired the first shot at Gettysburg, igniting the bloodiest three days in American history. Henry Jackson and Francis Fanness were part of the Thirty-seventh Illinois Infantry, and D. L. Boone was a recruit with the Forty-fourth Illinois Infantry. These units were also mustered into federal service in September 1861. The Thirty-seventh met the enemy on battlegrounds in Arkansas, Missouri, Mississippi, and Louisiana. The Forty-fourth also saw battle in Arkansas and Missouri in addition to Tennessee and Kentucky.

The Thirteenth Illinois Cavalry was organized in December 1861. Frederick Brinkman and brothers William and John Conrad Riegel joined this unit, which saw service in Arkansas and Missouri. By far, the largest number of local men, including Marquis Axtell, Nicholas Balzeger, Brock Frazier, Joseph Hunt and his nephew Carlos, and the Briggs brothers—Wesley, Joel, and Sidney—mustered into service with Company M of the First Illinois Artillery, which was organized in September 1862. The First Artillery saw service at Chickamauga and in many skirmishes in Georgia.

An Illinois Central engine typical of those in use during the Civil War

Illinois Central Railroad's depot in Thornton Station, later known as Homewood

Below: Henry Zimmer *(Cowing Collection)*

Unlike today, news of the war's progress spread slowly. Mail under normal circumstances could take a couple of weeks to reach its destination, and with complications created by the war, delivery times were even longer. The people of Thornton Station had somewhat of an advantage in this situation. The Illinois Central was the only railroad leading due south from Chicago during the war. It was the route of tens of thousands of soldiers and vast quantities of supplies going south and of wounded and furloughed soldiers moving north. Many times, news of events in far off places reached Thornton Station through passengers on these trains. This method, however, may not have been the best for accuracy.

It is likely this was the means of communication that convinced general store owner Henry Zimmer to move his merchandise into the country for safekeeping during July 1863. Zimmer had heard that Confederate General John Hunt Morgan and his troop of marauders known as Morgan's Raiders were moving north ransacking and burning whatever lay in their path. Fearing a complete loss of his stock, Zimmer moved quickly. Morgan and his men, however, never came anywhere near Thornton Station. His reign of terror was confined primarily to southern Indiana and Ohio where he was eventually captured by month's end.

Schoolhouse of the German School Association of Thornton Station, built in 1862 ***(St. Paul Community Church)***

Despite scares like this and other uncertainties caused by the war, residents of Thornton Station went about their daily activities as best they could. In 1862, during the depths of the war, the growing population of German immigrants formed the German School Association of Thornton Station to respond to the educational, cultural, and religious needs of their children. Most members had recently immigrated to the United States, and the school association was seen as a way to maintain a link to their homeland while learning to live in a new and foreign environment. A group of seventeen men met in April 1862 to form this association, and steps were taken to develop a constitution, obtain a qualified teacher, and purchase land to erect a schoolhouse.

The association purchased land from developer George Morris, and the lot selected was just west of what today is the intersection of Olive Road and Dixie Highway. The lot cost $42, and a frame school building, 40 feet long and 20 feet wide, was constructed on this land for $334. A man by the name of Gekler was hired to teach the schoolchildren in the German language, and he also delivered sermons on Sunday mornings in the schoolhouse.

By 1864, a dispute arose amongst members of this association, which ultimately led to its dissolution. The schoolhouse was put up for auction, and seven of the original organizers pooled their resources to purchase the building. These men, identified as William Gottschalk, Henry Windler, Christoph Mueller, Henry Zimmer, George Riegel, Frederick Schulz, and Frederick Hammer, were anchors of the commu-

nity, and through their efforts, the school operations continued, and eventually Thornton Station's second church, St. Paul Evangelical, was established. The new congregation selected Phillip Klein, a recent seminary graduate, as its first pastor, and he was instrumental in developing the church's constitution, which was signed by sixteen parishioners on May 21, 1865. In addition to the seven men listed above, Conrad Zimmer, John Puhrmann, J. Conrad Riegel, John Oberin, George Schmidt, Henry Heuer, Frederick Hildebrand, William Ohr, and Frederick Utermark helped to organize the new congregation. Descendants of many of these men still live in the community today.

Eight years later on November 23, 1873, members of St. Paul's dedicated a new church building, which had been constructed for about $3,000 on a parcel of land north of the German schoolhouse facing the Chicago-Vincennes Road. The church building included a steeple that housed a bell that for years rang out the call to Sabbath services, tolled for the death of church members, and sounded the alarm as Homewood's fire bell.

The spring of 1865 brought much for the residents of Thornton Station to be thankful for. They celebrated as the second church in their growing community became established, and they rejoiced as the long and painful war between the states had come to an end and, to paraphrase the lyrics from a song popular at the time, "Johnny" came marching home.

Interior view of the altar of St. Paul Evangelical Church

***Top:* St. Paul Evangelical Church, built in 1873**

As the war ended, veteran soldiers returned to Thornton Station changed by their experiences. Most had never traveled more than a half dozen miles from their homes, and their service in the war took them to places they would have otherwise never seen. Many participated in battles and events they would recount the rest of their lives. Some, like Benjamin Morris and Charles Gregory, lost their lives and would return only as memories.

Morris, son of miller George Morris, was captured by the Confederates in battle near Madison Court House in Virginia. He was last imprisoned at Andersonville, the notorious Confederate prison camp in Georgia. During the fourteen months this camp was open, forty-five thousand Union soldiers were confined there, and almost thirteen thousand died from disease, poor sanitation, malnutrition, or exposure. Morris died of pneumonia at Andersonville in July 1864. Gregory, though not a resident of town, was a member of the First Presbyterian Church of Thornton Station and was listed in church records as dying in Paducah, Kentucky, in the autumn of 1864.

Andersonville Prison Camp

Ceremonies held July 13, 2003, dedicating a marker commemorating Homewood's Civil War dead *(Richard Barr)*

John Conrad Riegel walks along a sidewalk adjacent to his home. *(Betty Mizevitz)*

Other veterans like J. Conrad Riegel and Henry Guenther were left with scars that constantly reminded them how much they had sacrificed. Riegel, who had enlisted in November 1861, would serve for only a few months before powder burns left him blinded in both eyes. He was discharged in May 1862 and returned to live on the family farm, which was bounded by what is now Willow Road on the north, 187th Street on the south, Loomis Avenue on the east, and Ashland Avenue on the west. Later, Riegel went to Ohio to learn the art of broom making, and he opened a broom factory in Homewood on Martin Avenue just south of Main Street (Ridge Road). In 1869, he married Rebecca Hart, thirteen years his junior and a daughter of pioneer settler James Hart. The couple would have four children, and their life was a happy one until tragedy struck again. In the fall of 1890, Conrad lost Rebecca and two of their children, Olive and Henry Louis, to diphtheria. Despite the heartache, Riegel persevered and married Adeline VanderWilligan in 1893. To this union, three sons were born, the last in Conrad's seventy-second year. The family's home was on the lot where the Starbucks Coffee Shop is located at 18051 Harwood Avenue. For years, Riegel was a familiar site to Homewood residents, making his way to his shop and through town lightly tapping his cane to guide his way. The last bugle call for this veteran sounded in October 1919, ending a long and remarkable life after eighty-four years.

Guenther, a recent German immigrant, enlisted in the army in 1862 at the age of twenty-two. He was mustered into Company G of the Sixty-fifth Illinois Infantry, which was accepted for federal service on May 1, 1862. He was wounded in action at Columbia, Tennessee, in November 1864 and lost his right leg. Guenther returned home after being discharged in July 1865 and married Sophie Jansen in December of that year. The Guenthers were parents of five children. For a number of years, Henry tried his hand at running a tavern and hotel on the northwest corner of Main Street (Ridge Road) and the Chicago-Vincennes Road (Dixie Highway). He would later engage in the insurance business and would retire from that profession. Guenther was well known throughout the township and was active in political affairs. He served as tax collector in Thornton Township in the late 1870s and 1880s, and he was elected in 1893 to serve as Homewood's first village clerk. He also served as village president after the death of Dr. William Doepp in 1897. Guenther passed away in March 1920 at the age of seventy-nine.

Adeline Riegel and son Everett ***(Betty Mizevitz)***

William C. Scupham *(Doris Waldschmidt)*

John Conrad and Adeline Riegel's sons—(front) Everett, Paul, and John C. Riegel; (rear) friends George Wesse and Bill Tolhurst *(Betty Mizevitz)*

Many other Civil War veterans moved into the community after the war, and these veterans were always present at Memorial Day services and Fourth of July events. The last two Civil War veterans living in Homewood were William Scupham and Joe Jones. Scupham was a private in the First Illinois Artillery when he was captured in the battle of Atlanta and imprisoned at Andersonville. After the war, he married Johannah Doepp, a daughter of Dr. Doepp, moved to Homewood, and operated a pharmacy in Chicago for forty years. He died in November 1924 at the age of eighty-one. Jones, affectionately known as "Uncle Joe," was a member of the United States Colored Troops. He was a pensioner from the Illinois Central Railroad and lived in Homewood for many years during his retirement. He died in December 1925. Jones was laid to rest at Mt. Glenwood Cemetery and accorded full honors at his service by members of the American Legion, Homewood Post 483. With these deaths, the era of the Civil War, after six decades, had come to a close in Homewood.

The Guenther home on the northwest corner of Main Street (Ridge Road) and the Chicago-Vincennes Road (Dixie Highway) *(Cowing Collection)*

Henry Guenther *(Village of Homewood)*

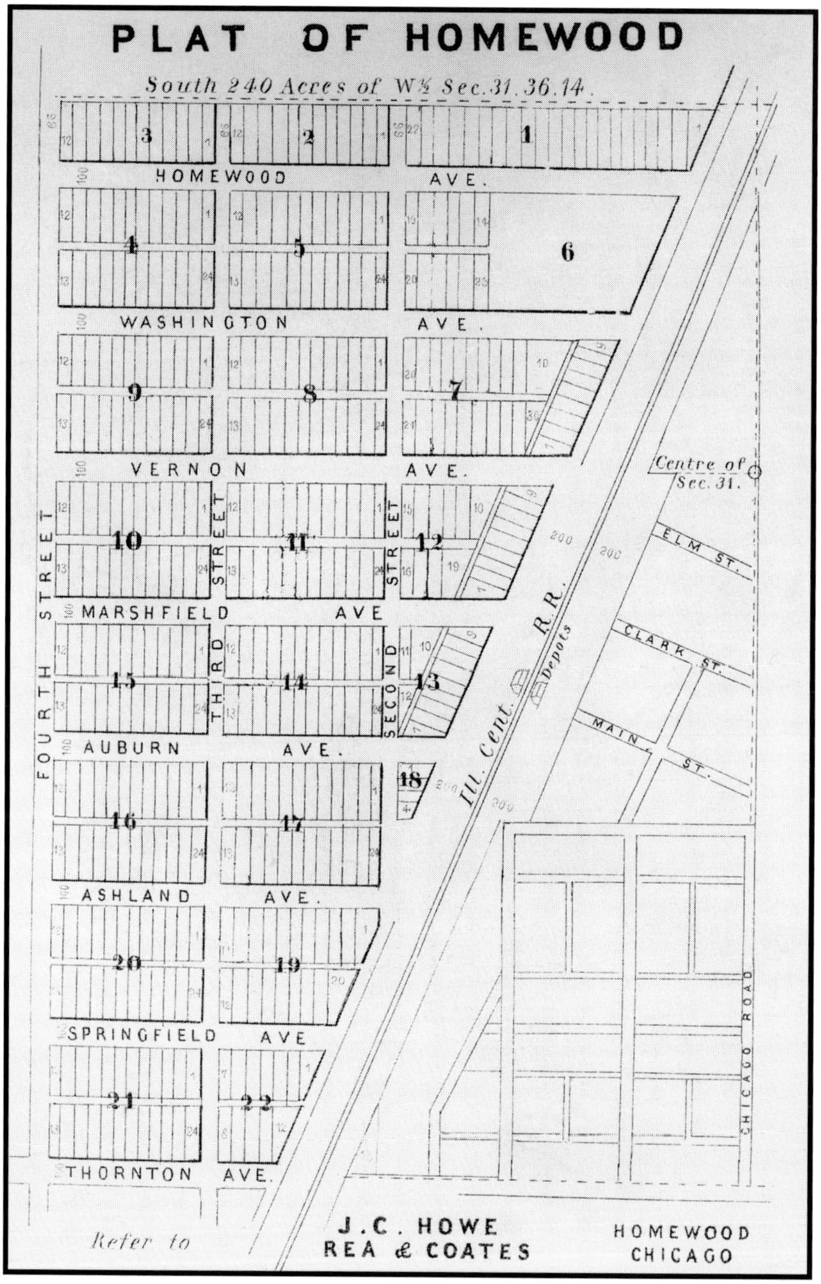

Plat of the subdivision Jabez Howe had planned on the west side of the Illinois Central tracks in Homewood in 1870. The development never materialized, and the area was eventually resubdivided. ***(Library of Congress)***

CHAPTER 4
A Village Blossoms

The end of the Civil War sparked renewed growth in Thornton Station. The 1867 edition of the *Guide to Illinois Central Lands* described Thornton Station as "23-1/2 miles south of Chicago, the area having a population of 500 which is steadily increasing. It has a Presbyterian church and a German church, two schools, a flouring mill, three hotels, two stores of general merchandise, two blacksmith shops and two wagon shops. A number of new houses are being built. There has been a demand for houses this past year, considerably in excess of the supply. The land in the region is good for grass, vegetable and dairy farming." Census data from 1870 further illustrates the growth the hamlet experienced after the war. These records indicate Thornton Station was also home to a butcher, a harness maker, two shoemakers, a tailor, and five, not three, hotel-tavern combinations.

The period after the Civil War was notable for another reason—a name change. A freight train wreck on the Illinois Central in 1866 provided the impetus for this change. Jabez C. Howe Sr. was a passenger on an Illinois Central train traveling from Clifton, Illinois, to Chicago when his train was delayed in Thornton Station by the wreck. Instead of resting in the shade or seeking refreshment in one of the nearby taverns, Howe spent his time exploring the region west of the railroad track that comprises much of what is now the west side of Homewood. Howe was so enamored with the countryside, he returned in 1868, purchased four hundred acres, and built a home for his family on land now known as the Governors Park subdivision.

Jabez C. Howe
(Cowing Collection)

View of the Locard family on the front porch of their home which was the "model" home Jabez Howe had constructed in his subdivision. The home still stands at 2137 Cedar Road.

Howe, like many of his neighbors, did not like the name Thornton Station. The village had grown over the years to where it was no longer just a stopping point on the way to "Old Thornton"; it was becoming the larger of the two communities, and the railroad ensured that growth would continue. Like Howe, many residents felt their town deserved a name of its own.

Others wanted a different name for more practical reasons. All too often, the similarity in names and the proximity in location caused much confusion, and the mail was frequently misdirected between the two communities. Although many residents wanted a new name, no one ever did anything to change it until Jabez Howe arrived.

In 1869, Howe circulated a petition among residents asking for the name to be changed to "Homewood," a name he thought was representative of the kind of town he hoped Thornton Station would grow to be—a community of homes surrounded by the beauties of nature. Howe presented the completed petition to Postmaster Henry Zimmer who sent it to Washington. Postal authorities there were amenable to the change, and by proclamation of the postmaster general, the name change took effect November 15, 1869. Thornton Station was now officially known as Homewood.

Howe worked to make his vision of Homewood become a reality. He subdivided the land west of the railroad track in the area of present-day Maple and Cedar Roads in residential lots in preparation for development. He planted elm, maple, and black walnut trees along the few streets he had laid out to give this area the "home in the woods" appearance he dreamed of. Howe even went as far as having a "model" home constructed for the grand sum of $2,000. Built in the early 1870s, this home still stands at 2137 Cedar Road. Howe saw promise in future development and wanted Homewood to become one of Chicago's most desirable suburbs.

Unfortunately, Howe's activities to place Homewood "on the map" were thirty to forty years ahead of their time. Home building in the area he developed did not take place on the scale he wished until after the turn of the century. Jabez Howe, however, had the foresight to see the potential in his new hometown, and his choice of a name for the town reflected that wisdom.

Strolling down the main streets of the community now known as Homewood, Howe and other residents could find businesses to take care of almost any need. A weary traveler waiting to make connections on an Illinois Central train or one passing through town on the Chicago-Vincennes Road (Dixie Highway) would have no problem finding suitable accommodations for an overnight stay. Old-fashioned hotels and saloons occupied the principal corners of the village. These establishments came alive on Friday and Saturday nights as townsfolk and farmers from the surrounding countryside visited them to enjoy weekly dances and a good dose of libation.

George Mertens' Grocery and Hardware Store located on the south side of Main Street (Ridge Road) east of the Illinois Central tracks

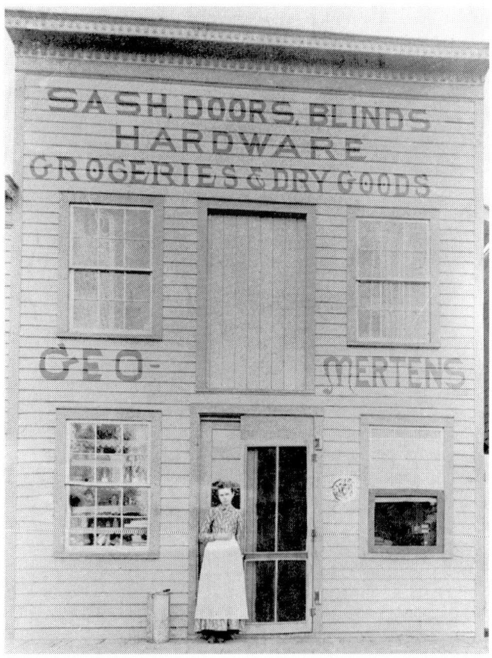

A short walk across from the rail depot on the southeast corner of Main Street (Ridge Road) and Morris Avenue (Harwood Avenue), the C. D. Robinson store was now a hotel and tavern owned by Johnny Ecker. Ecker operated this establishment through the late 1870s when a man by the name of Gottfried Voigtman took over. Voigtman ran the business until his death in 1885. Later that year, merchant George Mertens, who owned a hardware store next to Voigtman's, purchased the hotel and tavern. Over 130 years later, this site is still home to a tavern—the Ridgewood Tap.

On the north side of Main Street, several lots east of the Morris Avenue intersection, the Brinkman family continued to operate

The tavern on the southwest corner of the Chicago-Vincennes Road (Dixie Highway) and Main Street (Ridge Road) was built in the 1850s and was run by a number of owners including August Stommell, William Lehmke, and Gustave Beck throughout the years.

the hotel and tavern they opened in 1852. Henry Brinkman, the original owner, subsequently sold the business in 1859 to his brother Frederick, who operated it until his death in 1871, after which his wife Dora assumed full control. Large wagon sheds ran around the side and back of the Brinkman's saloon, and it was under these that farmers "parked" their rigs when they came in on Saturdays to visit the saloon and do their trading at local stores.

Two blocks east of the depot on the northwest corner of Main Street and the Chicago-Vincennes Road, Civil War veteran Henry Guenther operated his tavern and hotel, while across the street on the southwest corner of the same intersection, August Stommell ran a tavern and hotel through the late 1860s in a building built on this site. By 1870, Stommell had sold his place to William Lehmke who would operate a tavern here for over twenty years.

The largest saloon and hotel in Thornton Station was owned by Joseph Wolf and was located on the south side of Main Street a few lots east of Martin Avenue. Wolf had immigrated to the United States in 1848 and had settled on a farm in Bloom Township before moving into Thornton Station to open his place of business in the early 1860s. The large two-story frame building that housed his inn included seven sleeping rooms on the second floor, the tavern that occupied the front of the building on the first floor, and family living quarters to the rear on the first floor, which included two bedrooms, a parlor, kitchen, and dining room. Wolf ran the business until 1877 when his daughter, Helena, and her husband, Henry Moecker, took over. In 1885, the Moeckers sold the inn to William Gottschalk, who converted the building into a private residence for his family.

William Gottschalk and Henry Moecker stand in front of the Gottschalk home which had once been a tavern and hotel run by Joseph Wolf and Moecker. The home stood on the south side of Main Street (Ridge Road), a few lots east of Martin Avenue.

William Gottschalk and his family relax on the porch of their home. Son Henry is standing.

Gottschalk had immigrated to the United States from Germany in 1854 and had settled on a forty-acre farmstead adjacent to the land owned by Joseph Wolf. An industrious soul, William would eventually own over four hundred acres of farmland and six dwellings in town. In 1868, he began operating a hay-pressing business where hay was bailed for shipment by the railroad to supply the ever-increasing demand for hay by the Chicago stockyards.

Prior to the invention of "modern" hay-baling machinery, farmers had to bring their cut hay by wagonload to a local hay press to allow the hay to be baled for easy storage and shipment. A press usually consisted of a heavy wooden chamber about 2-1/2 feet x 3 feet wide and 10 feet deep. Loose hay was piled into the chamber, and a team of horses was hitched to a sweep arm attached to the chamber and walked in circles. This motion provided power, which would drive a wooden plunger attached to the sweep arm and compress the hay in the

William Gottschalk *(Donald Paden)*

chamber into tight bales. The bales were then bound by hand with wire.

To house this operation, Gottschalk built a huge barn, 40' wide by 180' long, west of the railroad track in the area where the Flosswood Condominiums now stand. In this barn, he placed a battery of hay presses and storage rooms for the baled product. A rail sidetrack ran along the barn, and every few days, boxcars were loaded on this siding, and the hay was then shipped to Chicago.

Apparently not busy enough with this business, Gottschalk, along with partner Henry Storch, started the operation of a brick and tile works just west of the hay barn several years later. The clay soil found there was perfect for the production of brick and drain tile, and four large round kilns were constructed to produce material year-round. As a distinctive mark, each brick made was stamped "HOMEWOOD" before being fired.

Far right: Christina Gottschalk *(Donald Paden)*

William and his first wife Christina had nine children including son Henry who would figure prominently in Homewood affairs throughout his life. Henry, born in 1864, took over operation of his father's hay presses in 1882. With youthful enthusiasm, he worked to increase the business further. He contracted with farmers throughout the surrounding area for almost every blade of hay available. In addition, he raised hundreds of tons of hay on farms he owned himself. At the height of his hay-pressing career, he owned

August Witt

Henry Gottschalk, on horseback, and brickyard workers, including many youths, pose with some of their handiwork.

820 acres of land, much of which was located in and around Homewood. Most of East Hazel Crest, Idlewild Country Club, and subdivisions like Southgate, Downey Manor, and Flossmoor Park was land once farmed by Gottschalk and his men. With all this acreage, output at his hay presses increased to four thousand tons per year.

Henry, like his father, wasn't satisfied with hay alone. In 1886, he purchased the brick and tile works from his father and Mr. Storch and with the same enthusiasm increased output there. The brickyard employed sixteen hands regularly, and the work force swelled to thirty–forty men in the summer months. Brick and tile were shipped by rail to points as far as Clifton and Chebanse on the Illinois Central. In the brickyard's best year, two hundred railcar loads of material were produced. Henry operated the hay-pressing venture for about fifteen years after which he turned management of the brickyard over to his brother-in-law, John Rabe.

Henry was not the only Gottschalk relation to do business in town. William Gottschalk also helped his sons-in-law establish themselves in business. August Witt married Marie Sophia Gottschalk in June 1876 and opened a grocery and dry goods store shortly thereafter in a building owned by his father-in-law. This frame structure still stands at the northeast corner of Ridge Road and Martin Avenue. Witt's grocery and dry goods store provided competition to the general store owned by Henry Zimmer farther west on Main Street and the store Civil War veteran Joel Briggs had started on Morris Avenue (Harwood Avenue) after his discharge from the army.

Workers pose for this picture taken outside of one of the brickyard's kilns.

After Witt's death from tuberculosis in November 1882, another Gottschalk son-in-law, William Winterhoff, took over trade at the store in December of that year. Winterhoff ran the store until 1885 when he and his wife Minnie moved to Lansing. The business was then sold to Henry Moecker while William Gottschalk retained ownership of the building. Moecker, like many of his counterparts in the business community, was actively involved in civic affairs in Homewood. He was elected to the school board and village board and was appointed postmaster of Homewood, serving in this capacity from 1885–1889 and 1893–1897.

August Witt's dry goods store was located on the northeast corner of Main Street (Ridge Road) and Martin Avenue. The building, renovated and enlarged over the years, still stands. *(Donald Paden)*

Other immigrants who settled in Thornton Station and Homewood in the 1860s and 1870s opened businesses that were important to the community. August Steiner, like William Gottschalk, emigrated from Germany in 1854. Steiner initially settled in Thornton Station but worked as a blacksmith and machinist in Chicago and many of the western states and territories before returning to Thornton Station to settle for good in 1859. He established a blacksmith shop here and concentrated on making plows, wagons, and farmer's implements. Steiner's shop was behind his home on Martin Avenue, south of Main Street. In 1880, Steiner purchased the Homewood Steam Flouring Mill from Nelson Seymour, who had purchased the mill from George Morris years before. Steiner made improvements to the mill and increased capacity to over seventy-five barrels of flour a day. In addition to grinding grain for local farmers, the mill also did "custom" work where railcar loads of wheat were brought in on an adjacent siding, milled, and sold to wholesalers, bakeries, and grocery and dry good stores in towns for miles around.

The milling process generated a large amount of unusable byproducts called "middlings." As the middlings made perfect fodder for livestock, the Steiners also raised 150–200 hogs a year in barns and feedlots next to the mill. August and his son Carl would own and operate the mill and feedlots for the next forty years.

Eliza and August Steiner *(Don Steiner)*

Given his background as a "smithy" and machinist, August Steiner was mechanically minded and quite inventive. Around 1880, he built Homewood's first fire engine, a small, four-wheeled, hand-drawn, hand-operated pump that

Pigs forage in the feedlot next to Steiner's Mill. ***(Don Steiner)***

Cornhusker patented by August Steiner ***(Don Steiner)***

was kept filled by a "bucket brigade." After over 120 years, this rig continues to be a prized possession of the fire department. Steiner operated one of the largest businesses in town and certainly had an interest in seeing the community had some sort of fire protection even though an organized fire department did not exist at the time. He also was the first in the village to have running water in his home. Behind his home, he constructed a two-story brick tower that contained a holding tank for water pumped into it by a windmill. Piping was installed from the tower to the house, and water flowed by gravity from the tower tank through the piping. Pressure was created to increase the water flow as a result of the height of the tank in the tower.

Steiner also received patents on a cornhusker/harvester in 1890 and improvements to it in 1894. This machine was one of the first successful mechanical harvesters, and representatives from the McCormick and Deering Reaper Works (predecessor to the International Harvester

William Buggert, left, and his father Christian stand in the doorway of their blacksmith shop with their family. As the signs attest, the Buggerts were also dealers for the Schuttler and Ottawa Wagon Companies and the Plano Harvester Machinery Company, a predecessor of International Harvester. ***(Barbara Kimport)***

Company) frequently came to Homewood to view the machine in use and consider purchase of the patent rights to it. Although the McCormick and Deering Company never did purchase the rights from Steiner, it is likely their employees gleaned many useful ideas to improve their harvesters during the visits they made to Homewood.

The daily grind of business did not preclude Steiner's involvement in other activities. He found time to serve as a school board member, Thornton Township trustee, and highway commissioner, and he was elected to serve as Homewood's first village president in 1893.

Steiner was not the only blacksmith to fire a forge in Homewood during these early years. Christian Buggert, another German immigrant, settled in Blue Island in 1852 and worked in a blacksmith shop there for a number of years. He later moved to Thornton Station in the late 1850s and built his home and shop on the southeast corner of Main Street and the Chicago-Vincennes Road. Buggert, later joined by his son William, operated here for decades, and his shop and large brick home were familiar landmarks to many as they passed through Homewood.

Like the blacksmith, many of the other businesses that populated the main streets of Homewood during this period are now considered relics of a bygone era. The harness maker, cobbler, and neighborhood butcher are just a few by name.

By 1865, master harness maker Fred Luekow was the proprietor of the small frame building on the northwest corner of Main Street and Martin Avenue that once housed the Alfred Robinson store.

Louise Duwe and daughter Eda stand in front of the family's harness shop, which was located on the northwest corner of Main Street (Ridge Road) and Martin Avenue. The Bank of Homewood occupies the site today. *(Gloria Sublette)*

Luekow sold the business and property in 1874 to another harness maker, William Duwe, who would ply his trade on this site until his death in 1920. For many years, Duwe worked on the first floor of this house while the second floor, which included two small bedrooms, served as home for his family that grew to include nine children. By the time of Duwe's death, the increasing popularity of the automobile had made the harness maker's job all but obsolete.

Cobbler Christopher Schroeder opened his shoe-making shop in the late 1850s and worked in Thornton Station through the 1860s. By 1865, Jacob Gold, another shoemaker, had settled in Thornton Station and made and repaired shoes in town through the late 1800s. By the turn of the century, most shoes were made in factories, leaving repair work the primary job of the local cobblers.

As mechanical refrigeration was nonexistent during these years, residents needed to shop for fresh meat on an almost daily basis. The needs of the community were served by butcher Fred Hammer who had operated a shop on Martin Avenue a block south of Main Street since the late 1850s. After Hammer moved from Homewood, Henry Stolzenbach bought the shop in 1881. To satisfy the desires of his customers, Stolzenbach purchased cattle, pigs, and chickens from local farmers and slaughtered some of these each day in a shed behind his shop. Stolzenbach, like many other businessmen, was also involved in village affairs. He was appointed village treasurer in 1902 and served in this position until his death in 1937. He also had the misfortune to fall from a railroad car in April 1915, crushing his left hand so badly under the wheels it had to be amputated. Despite this handicap, Stolzenbach continued to work in the butcher shop and manage village funds. Stolzenbach's sons, Albert and George, would follow their father into the business, and they operated the meat market through

Stolzenbach's butcher shop on Martin Avenue survived for over a century until it was torn down in 1997 to make way for a condominium project. *(Gene Roeder)*

the late 1940s. After this, Stolzenbach's shop served as home to a number of other businesses, and the building was a quaint reminder of Homewood's past for over a century. It was torn down to make way for a condominium project in 1997.

By 1880, continued growth in Homewood necessitated the construction of a larger public schoolhouse. During the 1870s, attendance at the old one-room schoolhouse had grown to over fifty students. For much of this decade, pupils in all eight grades were taught by the school's only teacher, a young man by the name of David Perry. A native of Beecher, Perry boarded with the Mitchell family in Homewood during the week and returned home to Beecher on weekends. As the school's only employee, Perry not only taught but also was responsible for all of the administrative and maintenance work at the school.

Students and teacher stand in front of Homewood's two-room schoolhouse built just north of St. Paul Church on the Chicago-Vincennes Road (Dixie Highway). The building, although extensively remodeled, still stands at 18120 Dixie Highway.

To alleviate overcrowding, a new two-room schoolhouse was built on the Chicago-Vincennes Road just north of St. Paul Church. Independence Park occupies a part of this site today. This lot was more centrally located and within easy walking distance for most children in the village. The two rooms required two teachers, and the 1880 census identified Oscar Andrews and Peter Lennon as the teachers residing in Homewood.

As the 1880s wound down, Homewood possessed many of the attributes of a desirable residential community. One attribute it did not possess, however, was a form of town government and many of the services that come with it. Progressive residents and businessmen were anxious to see this situation change and pushed for Homewood to incorporate. This movement would gain added momentum in the early 1890s.

Passengers await the arrival of an incoming train at the Homewood depot. The depot, located on the east side of the tracks, was well manicured, and was situated in a park-like setting for many years.

CHAPTER 5

Homewood Incorporates

As the decade of the 1890s dawned, the Illinois Central Railroad continued to be the major force in the growth and development of Homewood. A decision the railroad made in 1890 would solidify this position for decades to come.

The Illinois Central had initiated "suburban" or commuter rail service in 1856 between Chicago and Hyde Park (Fifty-first Street). Over the years, suburban service was gradually extended farther south and by the mid-1880s had reached the Dolton junction (138th Street). In April 1890, the railroad completed the installation of additional track to Harvey, a growing, planned industrial community founded by prominent Chicago lumber dealer, Turlington W. Harvey. By October 1890, track improvements were completed to Homewood, and a schedule of ten weekday suburban trains began operating between Homewood and Chicago on October 26.

James Cowing

That same year, James Cowing took over as the station agent for the Illinois Central. Cowing held this position for seventeen years and throughout this time lived on the second floor of the depot with his family. In his position as station agent, Cowing was responsible for receiving and dispatching the mail and all telegraph messages for the village. In 1899, Cowing's wife, Nellie, was appointed Homewood's postmistress, a job she held until 1925. After the turn of the century, the Cowings were also instrumental in the operation of Homewood's telephone exchange. For a time, it was said no message was sent from or received in Homewood without one of the Cowings handling it. Cowing became an important influence in Homewood affairs. He was elected village clerk in 1896 and served in this position for the next twenty-eight years. After leaving the railroad, he also became actively involved in real estate and banking activities in the village.

Nellie Cowing

Prior to the extension of suburban rail service, three long-distance passenger trains stopped in Homewood daily while heading north into Chicago. The frequency of trains to and from Chicago under the newly instituted suburban schedule proved to be a boon to the community. Villagers could now readily travel to Chicago to shop or conduct business at more convenient times. More importantly, the schedule was tailored to those who worked in the downtown and the outlying industrial districts of Chicago, which allowed these workers to easily travel to and from their places of employment. Because of this transportation improvement, Homewood became an attractive option for city dwellers looking to buy or build a home in a "country-like" setting. Homewood's destiny as a "bedroom" community was cast, and the town's population would double in each of the ensuing decades through 1930, except one.

Henry Gottschalk recognized that suburban rail service would not only be a great benefit to the village but would also provide a tremendous opportunity for him personally. Gottschalk tirelessly promoted the benefits of brick-building construction in efforts to increase business at his brickyard. In 1891, he constructed four identical two-story brick houses within the same block east of the railroad tracks on Maria Street

View looking east on Maria Street (183rd Street) from the railroad tracks shows the four identical homes Henry Gottschalk had built in 1891 of brick from his factory. A fifth home built the same year is visible in the distance.

(183rd Street). He hoped these houses would serve as a testament to the qualities of brick construction and would spur potential homeowners to build using brick. After construction, these buildings served, at various times, as housing for brickyard employees, as housing for visitors to the 1893 Chicago World's Fair who "commuted" to the fairgrounds via Illinois Central trains, and as rental homes. In later years, businesses occupied the first floors of these buildings while the second floors continued to serve as rental apartments. Today, two of the buildings still stand. One at 2135 183rd Street is home to Nix-Nax, and the Blueberry Hill Pancake House occupies the second at 2155 183rd Street.

Mrs. Dorthea Dorband stands in front of her home, built of "HOMEWOOD" brick by Henry Gottschalk in 1891. The home, now located at 2035 183rd Street, is the headquarters and museum of the Homewood Historical Society.

In addition to these structures, several other "HOMEWOOD" brick buildings were built in 1891. Gottschalk built two other brick homes that year that today are Homewood's only officially designated historic landmarks. One of these homes is commonly known as the Dorband-Howe House, located at 2035 183rd Street, and is now the headquarters and museum of the Homewood Historical Society. The second home, at 18101 Martin Avenue, has always been known as the Gottschalk House; Henry built this beautiful Queen Anne–style home for his family. A third building was built on the northeast corner of Main Street and Morris Avenue (Harwood Avenue) by Louis Mueller to house his hotel and saloon. Mueller had taken over the Brinkman hotel and tavern after Dora Brinkman died in 1886. The new tavern building he built, with its distinctive second-floor turret, was a Homewood landmark until 1965 when it underwent extensive renovations that included complete removal of the second floor and the turret.

Henry Gottschalk and his family stand in front of the magnificent home he had built in 1891 using "HOMEWOOD" brick. The home still stands at 18101 Martin Avenue.

Louis Mueller's tavern was another building built in 1891 of "HOMEWOOD" brick. The tavern was located on the northeast corner of Main Street (Ridge Road) and Morris (now Harwood) Avenue.

Louis Mueller stands with his son, Louis Jr., and patrons at the bar inside his tavern on Main Street (Ridge Road).

Top: Henry Gottschalk sits in the dining room of his home. His second wife, Sophia, is seated to his right holding their son Henry. Stanley Gottschalk is seated in the high chair.

Unfortunately for Gottschalk, aside from this spurt of brick construction, frame construction remained the most common home building method in Homewood until well after the turn of the century.

Wedding photo of Henry Gottschalk and his first wife, Anna Rabe

While Gottschalk initially believed the railroad's expansion would provide great opportunity, he soon realized it would be the source of extreme anguish. Sidewalks were almost nonexistent during this era, and streets were unpaved, making even short walks an unpleasant and muddy experience at times. It was not uncommon for pedestrians to walk amongst the railroad tracks whose rock ballast and wooden ties provided a relatively clean and smooth walking surface. This practice was dangerous when only one track ran through town, and the danger doubled after the second rail track was installed to accommodate suburban trains. On December 11, 1891, Gottschalk's wife Anna, his two-year-old daughter Lillian, and his sister Marie Witt were killed by a speeding train while walking home along the rail tracks after visiting friends. Marie Witt's daughter, Augusta, was the only one in the group to escape unharmed.

Marie Gottschalk Witt

Monument in Homewood Memorial Gardens to Marie Gottschalk Witt and Anna and Lillian Gottschalk

A front-page article in the December 12, 1891, edition of the *Chicago Daily Tribune* provided these details of the tragic accident that occurred the day before. "The women with their children started across the tracks at the crossing, 100' north of the whistling post at Homewood when a southbound freight came along. The engineer whistled and the women in their fright ran back on the northbound track and were caught by a Cincin-

Henry Gottschalk and his second wife, Sophia Rabe

nati fast express of the Big Four road. Augusta Witt was more active than her mother and cleared the track before the train reached the crossing. As the express shot past, the child turned and to her horror saw her mother and Mrs. Gottschalk thrown with terrible force a full thirty feet to the side of the track. Neither of the women were badly crushed but death must have been instantaneous, for they were dead before Engineer Ames and Conductor Andregg of the fast express reached them." Little Lillian Gottschalk was crushed to death by the impact with the train. The Big Four was the Cleveland, Cincinnati, Chicago, and St. Louis Railroad, which became a part of the New York Central and utilized the Illinois

Homewood's first village hall was built in 1894 on Clark Street (Chestnut Road). This photo was taken shortly before the building was demolished in 1938 to make room for the construction of the current village hall at 2020 Chestnut Road.

This view of St. Paul Church on the Chicago-Vincennes Road (Dixie Highway) shows the wood plank sidewalks and gas lamps installed throughout the village in the 1890s.

Central tracks north of Kankakee to reach Chicago. Compounding this tragedy was the fact that Mrs. Gottschalk was pregnant at the time of the accident, and Augusta Witt, her brother Theodore, and sister Louise were left orphaned.

Henry Gottschalk was devastated by these deaths. Although he would remarry in February 1895 to his wife's sister, Sophia Rabe, the first years after the rail accident were difficult ones. Gottschalk coped by immersing himself in business pursuits and civic affairs. One cause he worked hard to implement was the proposition of Homewood incorporating and forming a village government.

For years, Homewood residents had dealt with problems on their own or through public meetings. Some improvements were made by public subscription or through the generosity of leading citizens. Many improvements, however, went undone. Homewood lacked paved streets, sidewalks, and a water system. The town did not have police protection or an organized fire department. Homewood had long outgrown this method of governance, and the time had come for the community to have, at least, the basic municipal services.

By the fall of 1892, Gottschalk, Henry Moecker, and August Steiner had become the prime movers behind the incorporation efforts. They all agreed Homewood should have a village government, but they disagreed as to the territory the village should encompass. Gottschalk and Moecker believed the village should include the area from 175th Street to 183rd Street and from Western to Ashland Avenues, including a small section bounded by what is now Dixie Highway on the east, the

Henry Gottschalk (top) and August Steiner were both instrumental in organizing a village government. Steiner served as Homewood's first village president, 1893–1895, and Gottschalk served as village president from 1907–1908.

Illinois Central tracks on the west, and Birch Road on the south. Steiner, however, wanted the village to encompass all of the territory between 167th and 183rd Streets from Ashland to Western Avenues. Steiner pushed for inclusion of the area north of 175th Street, as he owned the 160 acres of land that comprises much of Calumet Country Club today.

Each side was adamant about the area the village should include, and both factions worked quickly to secure enough signatures on petitions to get their proposition on the ballot. The petitions filed first with the county would determine which proposal would appear on the ballot as the referendum question for the voters to decide.

Adequate signatures were obtained by each group at about the same time, and fate decided the outcome of which proposition appeared on the ballot. The Gottschalk-Moecker camp entrusted the U.S. mail to deliver their paperwork to the county clerk's office for filing. In those days, mail sacks were picked up "on the fly" by trains passing through Homewood, and the particular sack their petitions were in missed the train. Steiner, hearing word of this, took no chances and rushed to Chicago himself to deliver his petitions in person. Through this twist of luck, Steiner's proposition was the one that appeared on the ballot.

The referendum question was decided on February 11, 1893, and a total of seventy-two men (women could not vote) cast ballots. By a vote of forty-three "for" to twenty-seven "against" with two spoiled ballots thrown out, the referendum passed. Homewood would have a village government, and the village limits would extend north to 167th Street. Despite the struggle to include this section in the village, residents in the area north of 175th Street, then known as South Harvey and now a part of Hazel Crest, petitioned the village board for approval to de-annex from the village in 1895. The village board agreed to this, and six years later, in 1901, the residents of south Homewood, the area presently south of 183rd Street, north of Birch Road, west of Dixie Highway, and east of the I.C. tracks, successfully petitioned to be included in the village limits. In the end, the boundaries Gottschalk and Moecker envisioned became the actual limits of the village.

Election of the first village officers took place on April 18, 1893, and the Homewood Public Schoolhouse was the sole polling place. August Steiner was elected village president, Henry Guenther was elected to the village clerk's position, and the six trustees selected were Jabez Howe Sr., George Mertens, Nelson Seymour, Carl Puhrmann, Samuel Black, and Edmund Ball. William McClintock was elected to the position of police magistrate, a job alternately known as justice of the peace.

Wood plank sidewalks ended at the William Scupham home on the southwest corner of Olive and the Chicago-Vincennes Roads. The home was later moved to the southeast corner of Martin Avenue and Olive Road where it still stands as a classic example of Victorian architecture. *(Jean Ratko)*

The first village board meeting was held in the German schoolhouse, and subsequent meetings were held in the homes of Fred Puhrmann (located near where St. Joseph's parking lot now stands) and August Steiner until a decision was made on a new village hall. Building a village hall was the first major project the new board would tackle. Potential sites were scouted, and Henry Gottschalk even offered a vacant lot he owned in town for the building, provided it would be constructed of brick. For reasons unknown, the board did not accept his offer. After months of discussion, a lot was purchased from Sidney Briggs for $225 in December 1893. This parcel was located on Clark Street (Chestnut Road) west of the Chicago-Vincennes Road (Dixie Highway) and is the site of the current village hall.

Bids were solicited for construction of a two-story frame building 26' wide x 40' long x 22' high. Four bids were received, and W. J. Parnell was awarded the contract for $1,485 in January 1894. Construction proceeded rapidly, and the first village board meeting in the new building was held on April 30, 1894. Parnell must have done a credible job as he was elected to a village trustee's spot on April 17, 1894.

Although the village board debated for months on the details of construction of a village hall, there was little debate when it came to the question of sidewalks and other improvements.

For years, sidewalks in town were either nonexistent or installed randomly by a few conscientious home and business owners. Residents had grown weary of trudging around town through mud or dust, depending on what the weather conditions were. To remedy this situation, the village board passed an ordinance in July 1893 requiring landowners in what is now the area of the central business district to install "substantial" sidewalks fronting their property, built to specifications promulgated by the village. Property owners were given fifteen days from passage of the ordinance to have the sidewalks constructed themselves, or the village would have the work completed and assess the owner the cost. The sidewalks were to be "connective and constitute one system of uniform walkway." They were to be constructed on two-inch by six-inch piers to support two-inch by six-inch pine planks set four feet apart. On this base, "top-surfaced" pine planks, five feet four inches wide were to be placed. The ordinance further stated that the whole unit was to be properly nailed with 2-1/2-inch wire nails, no plank was to be over ten inches wide, and all lumber was to be of the grade called "good common." To forestall any shoddy workmanship, trustees Carl Puhrmann, Jabez Howe, and Samuel Black were appointed to monitor sidewalk construction and enforce the provisions of the sidewalk ordinance.

Following installation of the sidewalks, the village board turned its attention to street lighting. Other than light from lamps on private property, public ways were not lighted. In December 1894, twenty oil lamps were installed on principal corners throughout town. For most of the next decade, resident Billy Mueller was employed as the village's lamplighter. At dusk, Mueller was a regular sight, driving his two-wheel horse cart through town loaded with a small ladder, oil, and other supplies. At each lamppost, Mueller mounted his ladder, replenished the oil supply, trimmed the wick, and lit the lamp. For many of these years, he returned to the streets at 1:00 A.M. and extinguished the lamps to preserve oil. During the day, Mueller was also responsible for making repairs to the plank sidewalks. In later years, Mueller made a name for himself building new homes.

By 1896, the village board allocated funds to "pave" the first streets in Homewood. Main Street and the Chicago-Vincennes Road were the first two streets chosen. The pavement consisted of several layers of stone. Larger stone composed the base of the roadway, and this was followed by gravel. A final layer of crushed stone was placed on the road surface to provide for sure footing and a smoother ride. In succeeding years, additional streets were paved utilizing this method. One drawback to this was the dust the stone generated during dry spells. The dust churned up by passing wagon and buggy traffic was the bane of all homemakers trying to maintain a clean house. To combat this problem, oil was periodically spread on the streets in the warmer months to "keep the dust down."

In addition to these infrastructure improvements, the village board also addressed the police and fire protection needs of the community. After Homewood's incorporation in 1893, the board appointed a constable whose duties were to maintain the peace and enforce the laws and ordinances of the village. Except for handling an occasional petty break-in, little police work needed to be done, and the constable worked "part time" on an as-needed basis.

August Oberin was the first village constable appointed, and most of his time was spent breaking up fights and controlling inebriated revelers at village dances and picnics. Balls and dances were regular affairs held at village taverns through much of the year. After the Gottschalk Pavilion was built in the mid-1890s, this site became popular for many weekend dances, and the wooded grounds provided a fine grove for picnics. The Pavilion was built by Henry Gottschalk on land he owned, currently encompassing the Extreme Scene Skate Park south of 183rd Street on Harwood Avenue. It was one of the biggest halls in the surrounding area, and it could accommodate large crowds. This fact was not only a recipe for its success but also one for trouble.

Walter Gleason, Homewood's first full-time policeman, frequently patrolled the community on horseback. Gleason retired as chief of police in 1951 after serving in the position since 1904. *(Meyer Estate)*

Young "toughs" from other communities frequently "crashed" dances and picnics in town, which generally ended up in a fight between any number of the "out-of-towners" and the Homewood "boys." This problem became so commonplace, anyone sponsoring a large picnic or dance was required to get a permit from the village and pay a fee, part of which was used to hire a "special policeman" to patrol the event. The village board appointed a number of special policemen to assist the constable in controlling these affairs.

The Gottschalk Pavilion and grounds became a notorious venue for this type of hooliganism, and usually more than one special policeman was on hand to quell any disturbance. One classic example of these "troubles" occurred in September 1904, and a *Harvey Tribune* article told the story this way: "Lawrence Stringer, democratic candidate for governor of Illinois, visited Homewood last Saturday as advertised, and Jerry O'Rourke, township committeeman, killed the fatted

calf so that all who came to listen to Mr. Stringer might be fed. Kegs of amber fluid were also dispensed at the pavilion where the beef was carved. The mixture of Jeffersonian enthusiasm, roast beef and beer proved too strong for the crowd and the day ended in a disgraceful row, in which several dozens of Harvey and Homewood fellows got bruised bodies and disfigured countenances. Anticipating trouble whenever a crowd of Harvey fellows go out for a 'good time,' the Homewood authorities prepared for it by swearing in eight or ten special policemen to assist in preserving order." Despite police presence at these affairs, the fights continued but were usually broken up before they got too far out of hand.

This hand-drawn fire pumper served as the foundation of the village's firefighting efforts from about 1880 until 1907. The engine built by August Steiner is still a proud possession of the fire department today.

The area where the pavilion was located was called the "Bloody Fifth." Though the exact reason for the name is not known, it is likely a reference to the stained digits on the hands of the many pugilists who fought there.

By 1902, village fathers recognized the need for a full-time police officer, and Walter Gleason was hired for the job. Within a few years, Gleason was appointed to the post of police chief, a position he held until his retirement in 1951.

In addition to police protection, the village board concerned itself early on with preventing and controlling fire in the community. One of the first ordinances the board passed was entitled "An Ordinance Regarding Nuisances and the Prevention of Fire"; it outlined a number of conditions residents should follow for fire safety. Chief among these conditions was no one should "place, store or stack any hay, straw, fodder or any other combustible material inside the village within 200' of any building, house, store, barn or shed."

In July 1893, the board solicited volunteers in an attempt to organize a fire department. There was little interest amongst townspeople in this proposal as they appeared to feel the "old" method of fighting fires was fine enough. Since about 1880, after August Steiner built his hand-drawn fire pumper, this "engine" was housed in a small building near the intersection of Main Street and Morris Avenue (Harwood Avenue).

When a cry of fire was heard, all able-bodied men, women, and children turned out to operate the engine and form a bucket brigade to supply water to it.

Although the attempt to bring more structure to the firefighting efforts of the citizenry failed, the village board did appoint blacksmith William Buggert to the post of fire marshal and named Carl Steiner and William Duwe his assistants. These men were charged with the responsibility of directing the firefighting activities and, most importantly, were required to see to it that the Steiner hand pumper was maintained in good order and in a constant state of readiness.

In early 1896, a large fire consumed Homewood's first business buildings located at the southeast corner of Main Street and Morris Avenue, then occupied by a hardware store and a tavern owned by George Mertens. This disastrous fire served as the catalyst to renew efforts to organize a fire department. On January 6, 1896, an ordinance was passed establishing a fire department, and in a town meeting held on January 18, twenty-six men volunteered to serve in the department. William Buggert continued to serve as fire marshal, and by 1897, funds were appropriated to build a new fire barn to house the department's apparatus. This building was built on the village lot behind the village hall erected three years earlier.

As the 1890s drew to a close, Homewood residents could reflect with pride on the progress made in their community during the decade. Substantial improvements took place in the decade that served as a foundation for the growth and development that would occur in the village after the turn of the twentieth century.

New tavern and hardware store built by George Mertens in 1896 after the original buildings on the same corner, Main Street (Ridge Road) and Morris (Harwood) Avenue, burned down that same year.

Main Street (Ridge Road) looking west from the Chicago-Vincennes Road (Dixie Highway) around the turn of the twentieth century ***(Gloria Sublette)***

CHAPTER 6
A New Century

The decade following the turn of the twentieth century was one of tremendous technological change in Homewood and the rest of the country. Many of the basic conveniences taken for granted today, like electricity, telephones, and the automobile, were introduced to Homewood during this period. The pace of life quickened with these conveniences, which helped to bolster continued growth and development in the village. Homewood was no longer a frontier outpost; it was becoming a proper little suburban community, and new businesses like the village's first bank, which opened during the decade, provided evidence of this.

Although Thomas Edison completed the first commercial electrical generating station in New York City in 1882, the first house in Homewood did not have electricity until the mid-1890s. The Doepp family home and grounds were the first to be wired and lit with electric lighting, and young Herman Doepp was in charge of the small DC plant on their property that generated power for the lights. Following in Herman's footsteps, August Steiner's son, Henry, supervised the installation and operation of a generating plant that provided electric power to their home on Martin Avenue.

Herman Doepp

Both men saw the economic potential in providing electricity to the community and were keenly interested in developing the capability to do so. At the turn of the century, larger electric utilities, like the Chicago Edison Company and the Commonwealth Electric Company, who merged to form one company in 1907, were concentrating their efforts on servicing the businesses and residences of the city of Chicago. Other

Main Street (Ridge Road) looking east to Martin Avenue after the turn of the twentieth century. ***(Susan White)***

Below: **After the turn of the century, Theodore Witt was operating the dry goods and general store on the northeast corner of Main Street (Ridge Road) and Martin Avenue.** ***(Donald Paden)***

cities and towns in the outlying areas surrounding Chicago were being served by a plethora of smaller utilities operated by municipalities or local entrepreneurs. In Homewood, Herman Doepp convinced the village board to grant him an exclusive franchise to generate and distribute electricity throughout the village. The franchise was approved in February 1902 for a term of forty years. The agreement contained the important stipulation requiring Doepp to have his plant and distribution system up and running within fourteen months. Doepp soon realized the logistics and infrastructure needed to even power a town as small as five hundred people was much more complicated than providing electricity for the family estate. By May 1902, the village and Doepp agreed to cancel the franchise, which was subsequently awarded to the Calumet Electric Lighting Company, a predecessor of the Public Service Company of Northern Illinois, which later was taken over by the Commonwealth Edison Company.

Calumet Electric Lighting worked quickly to complete its distribution network in Homewood, and the village was one of its first customers. In August 1902, trustees voted to wire the village hall for electric lights, and in September, the village installed electric arc lights in the business district, replacing the oil lamps

erected less than ten years before. Within a few years, the village had placed electric lights at most of the major intersections in town, and many residents and businesses were converting their buildings to electricity. The days of gas and oil lamps were coming to an end.

After the turn of the century, the telephone, the invention Alexander Graham Bell patented in 1876, also made its first appearance in Homewood. The Chicago Telephone Company, which was established in 1878, opened an exchange in Homewood in 1901. The exchange was located in the building the Gottschalks owned on the northeast corner of Main Street and Martin Avenue, occupied at the time by a general store operated by Theodore Witt, Henry Gottschalk's nephew. Witt's sisters Louise and Augusta helped run the store and were also in charge of operating the telephone switchboard. The switchboard at the exchange was given Homewood telephone number "1," and succeeding businesses located in the building through the 1950s maintained this number and proudly touted it in their advertising. The Homewood Country Club was purported to be the first customer of the telephone exchange, followed by the Ravisloe Country Club and the Homewood Village Hall where a telephone was installed in the clerk's office in September 1901.

Theodore Witt *(Donald Paden)*

Louise Witt *(Donald Paden)*

Left: **Augusta Witt** *(Donald Paden)*

By 1908, James Cowing had taken over as manager of the Homewood exchange, and his wife Nellie, the village's postmistress, was also the exchange's chief switchboard operator. That same year, Cowing had a one-story brick building constructed on Main Street, and he rented the east half to the telephone company and the post office for their use while the west half was rented to F. J. Egan for his barber shop. A second story was added to this building, which still stands at 2048-50 Ridge Road, in 1917. The Chicago Telephone Company acquired other companies in northern and central Illinois and changed its name to Illinois Bell in 1920.

View of Main Street (Ridge Road) looking west towards Martin Avenue and the railroad tracks at the end of the street. Note the buggies and delivery wagons in front of the Witt Store on the right. *(Gloria Sublette)*

Postmistress Nellie Cowing stands at left in the doorway of the Homewood Post Office on Main Street (Ridge Road). The building still stands at 2048 Ridge Road.

In addition to electric and telephone service, mains were laid throughout the community in 1907 to provide gas for home heating. The Northwestern Gas Light and Coke Company was given a forty-year franchise to provide thc gas in Homewood. Northwestern merged with the Public Service Company of Northern Illinois in 1913, and the gas distribution business was spun off in 1954 to create the Northern Illinois Gas Company.

With the advent of electrical service in the area, Homewood was the beneficiary of a major transportation improvement. As early as December 1904, representatives of a Chicago investment group were in the area surveying land for an electric interurban railway that would travel from Chicago to Kankakee by way of Blue Island, Harvey, and Chicago Heights. Promotion of the railway, known as the Chicago &

Southern Traction Company (C&ST), was successful, and construction of the line started in 1905. As surveyed, tracks were laid east of Homewood on a right-of-way parallel to the west side of Halsted Street. Track construction was completed to Chicago Heights in June 1906, and the first trolley trip from Harvey to Chicago Heights took place on June 13. The fare for this trip was ten cents, and a round trip from Chicago Heights to the line's terminus in Chicago at Seventy-ninth and Halsted Streets cost forty cents. Track installation was completed to Kankakee in November 1907, and by 1912, the Chicago terminus had been extended to Sixty-third Street.

Near Homewood, the Chicago & Southern Traction Company built a small depot at the intersection of Halsted Street and Thornton Road (Ridge Road). The area around the depot was unincorporated and was known as

Early Chicago & Southern Traction streetcar stopped near the Franklin depot located on the northwest corner of Main (Ridge Road) and Halsted Streets. Henry Axtell is sitting in the back of the car. ***(Wendell Axtell)***

Top: **Advertisement of the Chicago & Southern Traction Company**

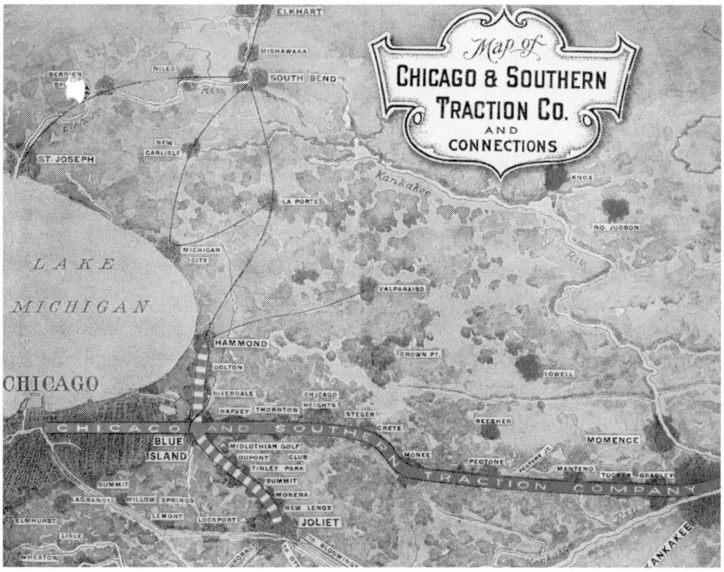

Franklin, named after Franklin Axtell who had owned a farm near the depot. This stop served passengers who walked to and from downtown Homewood and also served mourners who attended burials at the cemeteries east of the intersection. A special funeral car that carried both passengers and casket made these trips. Farther south, another depot was built near the intersection that today is known as 187th and Halsted Streets to serve the Glenwood Manual Training School.

Map showing the route of the Chicago & Southern Traction Company ***(Myron Tibbe)***

The interurban was never a financial success and would enter into receivership twice during its existence. The first receiver was appointed in October 1911, and through his efforts, the Chicago City Railway purchased all C&ST lines within the city of Chicago while a new company named the Chicago & Interurban Traction Company (C&IT) was formed to operate the C&ST lines outside the city limits.

By 1922, operating costs kept climbing, red ink continued to flow, and a receiver was again appointed to oversee operations. Subsequent service cuts and fare increases saved money but created ill will among customers. Further complicating matters was the completion of the Dixie Highway in 1921. This concrete road, which paralleled the interurban's right-of-way in many areas, allowed buses to compete for passenger traffic and motor trucks to compete for the interurban's freight traffic. The completion of the Illinois Central's suburban line electrification in 1926 sealed the C&IT's fate, and the railway ceased operating on April 23, 1927.

Another factor contributing to the demise of the interurban was the rising popularity of the automobile. At the time of the interurban's first trip through the area, the automobile was an expensive novelty for the rich. Early "horseless carriages" lived up to their name. They had high wheels, the look of a fancy horse buggy, and were crafted individually using many of the same materials carriages were made of. It wasn't until Henry Ford fully instituted the assembly line method of production in 1913 that the automobile became affordable for the masses. This dramatically increased Detroit's output of automobiles, and more cars meant less people riding the interurban.

In Homewood, Dr. William Doepp II was the first to own an automobile—a 1908 model manufactured by the Schacht Motor Car Company of Cincinnati, Ohio. The following year, Henry Gottschalk became the second in the village to own an automobile with his purchase of a thirty-horsepower 1909 touring car manufactured by the Moline Automobile Company of East Moline, Illinois. Grocer Henry Funk and businessman Fred Gold followed with automobile purchases shortly thereafter. Despite these purchases, it would be a number of years before there would be a significant number of autos owned by Homewood residents. The horse would serve as the prime mode of transportation in town well into the teens, and a business, the Homewood Stock Farm owned by Louis Metz and his family, capitalized on this.

Metz moved to Homewood in 1901 and was a breeder and importer of Percheron and Belgian draft horses. These breeds of horses were the favorites of farmers and teamsters who moved freight on streets around the country. Metz owned property southwest of the brickyard, in the area where Walt's Food Store is now located. He imported dozens of horses at a time from France and Belgium for sale and breeding. Horses he bred were shown at fairs and exhibitions

Lucy Funk and friend sit in her father's Case automobile. Henry Funk was one of the first to buy a car in Homewood. ***(Alvin Henke)***

Advertisement for the Metz's Homewood Stock Farm located on land now south of 183rd Street and east of Western Avenue. *(Breeder's Gazette)*

throughout the Midwest, and many were prizewinners. Metz developed a fine reputation, and his stock was well sought after. His business prospered up until his untimely death in 1938. Ironically, after years of working with large draft horses, Metz was killed after being kicked by a team of mules, a breed he began to raise in later years.

Proof of prosperity in Homewood also came in more tangible ways. During the decade, a brick schoolhouse was built, the village's first bank opened, and other new businesses were started in town.

In 1904, Homewood School Board members realized that the growing population of school-age children in town was overwhelming the two-room schoolhouse built some twenty years before. A referendum to approve a $10,000 bond issue to finance a new building was held and passed by a large majority. Construction of a handsome two-story brick building, known as the Standard School, was completed during the summer of 1904. The school building consisted of four large, airy classrooms with plastered walls, wood wainscoting, hardwood floors, two center cloakrooms, an office, an attic, and a basement. The school opened with 117 pupils in eight grades. Mr. Herman J. Broek was principal, and he shared teaching duties with Emma Mullen. Students interested in attending high school rode the train to Thornton Township High School in Harvey, which opened in 1899.

As construction of the new schoolhouse was to take place on the site of the old one, that building was sold to Billy Mueller, who moved it a lot to the north. Mueller then remodeled and converted the old schoolhouse into apartments. It was further altered in ensuing years, and today stands at 18120 Dixie Highway, housing businesses like Bannon Floor Coverings on the first floor and apartments on the second floor.

Four years later, Henry Gottschalk, along with his brother-in-law John Rabe, James Cowing, and Henry Moecker, established the Homewood State Bank. Construction of a two-story brick building was completed on the southeast corner of Main Street and Martin Avenue (2025 Ridge Road), and the bank opened its doors on October 1, 1908. Day-to-day business was conducted by Henry Gottschalk, the bank's president,

Standard School was built in 1904 on the Chicago-Vincennes Road (Dixie Highway) just north of the St. Paul Church.

and by James Cowing, who served as the bank's cashier. Deposits were strong, and the people of Homewood were proud that their town could support a growing financial institution. The building also had space for a retail store at the rear on the Martin Avenue side. In this space, Arthur Farr opened a dry goods store specializing in men's, ladies', and children's clothing.

Standard School's first graduating class (1905): Fred Borgwardt, Eleanor Howe, Lulu Schutius, Marguerite Schellenbarger, Myrtle Harwood, Flossie Van Gunter, and Frank Cowing. *(Cowing Collection)*

Farther west on Main Street, Henry Funk purchased the buildings on the southeast corner of Morris Avenue (Harwood Avenue) that George Mertens had built after the original structures were destroyed by fire in 1896. On the corner, Richard Stogentine operated a tavern and rooming house/hotel, and next door to the east, Funk opened a store specializing in "fancy and staple groceries, hardware and graniteware." Across the street, Clara Nieburger, daughter of harness maker William Duwe, opened an ice cream, candy, and card shop in Henry Zimmer's building after he retired in 1908.

On the south side of town, Maria Street (183rd Street) was also becoming popular as a place to establish a business. Widow Bertha

Homewood State Bank, the village's first bank, was built in 1908 at the corner of Main Street (Ridge Road) and Martin Avenue. The building still stands at 2025 Ridge Road. *(Gloria Sublette)*

Check drawn on the Homewood State Bank *(Rudy Schreiber)*

Heuer purchased a brick cottage on Maria Street in 1901 and began to sell groceries out of the front room to support her family. After a few years, she had a fine two-story brick building built to house her business, the South End Grocery, on the first floor and to provide living quarters for her family on the second floor. Years later, William Lassen purchased the building and assumed the operation of a tavern that Leonard and Ethel Schoof had started in the building years earlier. In 1969, Lassen planned on expanding the building, and after workers started excavating for a new foundation adjacent to it, the structure partially collapsed, and the building had to be completely demolished. A new building was built in 1970 that still houses Lassen's Tap at 2131 183rd Street.

In 1908, William Brutlag built a two-story building several lots east of Heuer's store on the southwest corner of Maria Street and Morris Avenue where he operated a tavern on the first floor and maintained his residence on the second floor. Brutlag did a good business on the "south end" of town as all his competitors—Richard Stogentine, Louis Mueller, and Robert Starkman, who was now running the tavern on the southwest corner of Main Street and the Vincennes Road—were all within two blocks of each other "up town" on Main Street.

Rounding out the business enterprises on Maria Street were florist Louis Schoof, who lived and worked on the northwest corner of Maria and Morris Avenue, and Fred Tatgenhorst, who opened his first barbershop, complete with bathtub, in 1909. After establishing a loyal clientele, Tatgenhorst moved his shop in 1913 to a building he purchased on Main Street.

Other men who lived in the village operated home delivery businesses that contributed to the "modern" conveniences in the community. After the turn of the century, fewer people living in town had milk cows of their own, and there was no dairy operation in Homewood. Young Henry Fiebig filled this void as the local deliveryman for the Harvey Pure Milk Company. Each morning, Fiebig picked up milk at the rail depot that had been shipped from the dairy in Harvey. Fiebig would then make his deliveries, door to door, using a horse-drawn wagon. At each home, he either met the housewife at the door with her pitcher in hand, or he filled a pitcher she left by the door with a note on it as to the amount of milk needed. With a 2-1/2-gallon galvanized can and quart measuring tin, Fiebig carefully filled the pitcher to give the customer the desired amount. After a few years, Christ Schimmels took over the route, delivering milk in bottles by then. Schimmels, always prompt and courteous, had the town in an uproar one Monday in October 1910. Housewives all over Homewood waited throughout the day for a milk delivery that never came. On the job early the next

Henry Funk stands on the steps of his grocery store on the south side of Main Street (Ridge Road).

Bertha Heuer's South End Grocery Store on Maria (183rd) Street *(Bert Heuer)*

William Brutlag, center in white, and patrons stand outside his tavern located on Maria (183rd) Street and Morris Avenue.

morning, Schimmels explained he had gotten tired of the single life, married a fine lady on Sunday, and took Monday off for a honeymoon. Everyone seemed to understand.

By the mid-teens, the dairy built a building, under the name of the Homewood Milk Company, on the Dixie Highway north of St. Joseph's Church, and John Overtoom was in charge of the dairy's delivery operations, which had expanded due to Homewood's increasing population. The Dixie Dairy Company purchased the Harvey Pure Milk Company in 1921, and the Homewood Milk Company facility closed and consolidated with Dixie's Harvey and Chicago Heights operations. Home milk delivery was a godsend to all the housewives and children who dreaded spending cold winter mornings in the barn milking old "Bessie."

Ed Bang was another resident who delivered a commodity that was crucial to the health and well-being of the community—ice. Prior to mechanical refrigeration, ice was indispensable as a means of keeping meat, dairy products, and other foods fresh and edible for any period.

Henry Fiebig in his milk delivery wagon. The small boy is Henry's brother Harry.

Ice delivery wagon of the Homewood Coal, Ice and Material Company

Maintaining a supply of ice in the winter was generally no problem; however, keeping a supply available in the summer, when it was really needed, was much more difficult. Bang accomplished this by building several icehouses in the village. The icehouses were basically large storage barns, the walls of which were heavily insulated with cork or sawdust. In these, Bang stored blocks of ice he and his crews cut from ponds and waterholes in Homewood. These blocks were then layered in the icehouses, and sawdust was spread between each layer as additional insulation. Properly prepared, ice could last well over a year. Bang and his men would then deliver ice throughout town, stopping at homes displaying an ice card. The card had numbers at each corner indicating a specific amount in pounds. The number displayed upright at the time the ice wagon passed was the amount of ice delivered to the home and placed in the family's "ice box."

Bang had several icehouses built in Homewood. One was just west of the Steiner mill, and a second was adjacent to a waterhole where ice was harvested near the present-day intersection of Harwood Avenue and Willow Road. Bang also purchased the grounds of the brickyard

William Brutlag, left, and patrons inside his tavern where one window advertised the place as the "Hunter's Headquarters."

Fred Tatgenhorst inside his barber shop on the north side of Main Street (Ridge Road) east of Martin Avenue.

from Henry Gottschalk in 1917, and the expansive hole where clay was taken to make bricks served as an excellent source of ice when filled with water. A large lumber-storage shed on the grounds was converted and used as his third icehouse. In addition to these, Bang supplied ice to the private icehouses in town owned by saloonkeeper Louis Mueller, butcher Henry Stolzenbach, and grocer Henry Funk.

As if home delivery of milk and ice was not enough, the United States Post Office approved rural free delivery for the areas surrounding Homewood in December 1904. The first home mail deliveries for those living outside of town started on January 2, 1905. Homewood resident Edwin Buell was the carrier hired to make these deliveries. A tremendous convenience for rural residents, those living in town still had to visit the post office to pick up their mail for almost another quarter century.

By 1910, Homewood lacked one utility essential to the health and safety of its residents—a municipal water system. A waterworks was not only necessary for a dependable supply of clean and potable drinking water, it was also necessary as a source of water for the village's fire protection needs. Although this issue had been discussed for years, the village could no longer afford to delay action. A referendum was held in September 1910, and voters were asked to approve a $5,000 bond issue for the construction of a water well, pump house, and storage tank. The result was a resounding "yes" with 116 votes cast in favor of the proposal to 14 votes against.

After this, the village worked quickly to complete the system. Contracts were let in October for an 80,000-gallon water tank and tower and for the drilling of a 10" well. This work was completed in February 1911, and the well extended 250′ below ground and supplied water at the rate of 175 gallons per minute. A contract for laying water pipes throughout the village was let in July 1911 at an additional cost

Ed Bang, his daughter Frances, and F. O. Multog stand alongside one of the ponds Bang used to harvest ice in the winter months. *(Elaine Baker)*

Aerial view of downtown Homewood

Village President Louis Mueller, in suit, and Henry Moecker to his right look on as water is pumped testing the village's first well in 1911. *(Cowing Collection)*

of $21,811, which was paid through a special property tax assessment. By the end of 1911, the system was complete, and thirty-five fire hydrants and 26,037 feet of water mains were in place and were supplied by the pump house and water tower located behind the village hall. Police Chief Walter Gleason was given the added duty of overseeing the water works, and he acted in the dual capacity of water superintendent and police chief for the next twenty-five years.

Residents eagerly tapped the mains and installed pipes in their homes for running water. Fire Chief Fred Gold, later the village president, was the village's first residential customer, and the Illinois Central Railroad was the first commercial account and ultimately the village's largest water user. By August 1913, the village was pumping over 700,000 gallons of water per month to meet consumer demands. The turn of a faucet handle was so much easier than pumping water by hand from the family well.

Conveniences meant more time for leisure activities, and one leisure pursuit spawned major changes in Homewood during the decade as large sections of agricultural land in or surrounding the village were converted to uses of a new "industry"—golf.

The Fred Gold Home on the Chicago-Vincennes Road. The home is now Ryan Funeral Home at 18022 Dixie Highway. ***(Cowing Collection)***

Inset: **Fred Gold** ***(Gloria Sublette)***

John Schultz was operating a tavern and hotel catering to golfers visiting the courses in the area under the name of the Hotel Golf in 1910 at the southeast corner of Main Street (Ridge Road) and Morris (Harwood) Avenue. *(Gloria Sublette)*

CHAPTER 7
Fore!

Golf, the ancient Scottish pastime, was introduced in the United States during colonial times. The first known golf club in the U.S., the South Carolina Golf Club in Charleston, was established after the Revolution in 1786. It wasn't until the 1880s that the game gained in popularity, and many courses sprang up around the country. In the Chicago area, the first courses were not established until the 1890s, and the earliest ones included the Chicago Golf Club in Wheaton (1892), the Downers Grove Golf Club (1892), the Riverside Golf Club (1893), and the Onwentsia Club in Lake Forest (1895).

In the area south of the city, the Illinois Central Railroad served to facilitate development of these courses in the "country." Prior to the widespread use of the automobile, the train was the quickest and most reliable form of transportation. Homewood, being the end of the line for suburban service, was a logical place for golf club promoters to scout for large tracts of relatively inexpensive land close to the rail line. The vast amounts of hayfields under cultivation around Homewood also made the area attractive as this acreage could easily be converted for recreational uses.

By 1910, three golf clubs were operating in or adjacent to the Homewood village limits. The clubs provided a huge economic boost to the community. In addition to employing dozens of tradesmen and laborers to construct the clubhouses and ancillary buildings, caretakers and painters were employed to maintain them after construction. Groundskeepers were constantly kept busy during season, grooming and manicuring the courses and landscaping. Cooks, kitchen help, and wait staff were needed to prepare and serve meals in the dining rooms and at the many parties held throughout the summer months. Teenage boys also earned money caddying at the courses after school, on weekends, and during summer vacations. Most of those employed were Homewood residents.

Aside from those directly employed by the clubs, many affluent members built summer homes surrounding the course grounds. Local carpenters and construction crews were hired to build these homes, and handymen, gardeners, and domestic help were employed at most of them, further increasing the employment opportunities for Homewood residents.

The seasonal increases in Homewood's population also meant added patronage for just about every business in town. The butcher, baker, grocer, and even the tavern owners were all happy to usher in the golfing season each year.

The first golf club established in our area was the Homewood Country Club, officially chartered in October 1899. The club was the brainchild of several Hyde Park businessmen enamored with the game and convinced that the "south side" needed a club of its own situated along the Illinois Central line. The Midlothian Country Club had been organized a year earlier, on the Rock Island rail line, but it was not easily accessible to those living in Hyde Park and other districts south of Chicago.

John Gilchrist and Fred Jenkins, executives with the Edison Company, along with other businessmen including John Wallace, John Nellegar, and Robert Wells, explored the area around Homewood during

Clubhouse of the Homewood Country Club built in 1900 near the present-day intersection of Flossmoor Road and Western Avenue ***(Chicago Historical Society)***

The Illinois Central named the stop that served the Homewood Country Club "Flossmoor." This depot, located on the east side of the tracks, was completed in 1900. ***(Flossmoor Public Library)***

the summer of 1899, in search of the perfect spot to build their golf club. To aid in this endeavor, the men engaged Frank Riedle, a Chicago real estate agent who was fluent in German. Riedle assisted in negotiating land options with several of the German farmers in the area. Riedle would subsequently move to Homewood and would open a real estate office in town. Through the years, he would become so well respected, a street was named in his honor after his death in 1917.

Gilchrist and his group were shrewd businessmen. They had placed three properties around Homewood under option, including the Sidney Briggs farm located west of the Illinois Central tracks and north of Maria (183rd) Street. Gilchrist had also scouted the August Hecht and Christ Hibbing farms south of Homewood and liked what he saw. Both parcels were south of today's Flossmoor Road; Hecht's parcel lay east of what is now Western Avenue while Hibbing's was on the west side of that roadway and east of the I.C. tracks. Their property had an undulating appearance, and a creek named for one of the area's first settlers, Benjamin Butterfield, meandered through it. Gilchrist knew this was the land he wanted for the club. At first Hecht and Hibbing were unwilling to give an option on the land except at an unreasonable price per acre. When apprised of the other parcels under option around Homewood, both men became more amenable to negotiating. They both ultimately executed contracts to sell 160 acres each to the fledg-

View from what today is Flossmoor Road looking north to the Flossmoor depot *(Illinois Central Historical Society)*

ling club for the sum of $125 an acre—a price just a tad above the $1.25 an acre the property sold for in the late 1830s!

After the land acquisition was completed, club members hired Herbert J. "Pops" Tweedie in the spring of 1900 to design the layout of the course on Hecht's acreage, and John Pearson was hired as the club's first professional. Construction was completed that year on the first clubhouse, a large two-story frame structure located southeast of the present-day intersection of Flossmoor Road and Western Avenue. This site was selected because it was the highest piece of ground on the property and had a commanding view of the rest of the course. Keeping a promise made to Gilchrist earlier, the Illinois Central also extended suburban rail service to Illinois Street, now known as Flossmoor Road, and completed construction there of a station they named "Flossmoor" in April 1900.

As part of the land deal, Hibbing's 160 acres were subdivided into residential lots, and many were sold to club members who built summer homes on them for their families. These large "cottages," converted to all-season houses long ago, are easily recognizable today as one drives through the neighborhood west of the country club grounds.

The club developed a good reputation from the start. It hosted a number of early amateur tournaments and was the site of the 1906

Homewood Country Club's second clubhouse was completed in 1908. Like the first clubhouse, this building was struck by lightning and burned down in 1914. Shortly thereafter, the construction of the third and present clubhouse was started in a different location, and the club officially changed its name to the Flossmoor Country Club.

Western Open. Things went well for the new club until lightning struck the clubhouse in May 1907 and completely destroyed the building. A second clubhouse was built on the same site and was completed in October 1908. This brick and cement building was thought to be fireproof. Contrary to the old adage, lightning did strike twice, and the second clubhouse was leveled after the roof caught fire in a May 1914 electrical storm, and the fire spread throughout the rest of the building. Hoping to prevent further trouble with Mother Nature, club officials built the third and present clubhouse about a half mile south of the original site—a move they haven't regretted since the clubhouse was completed in 1916.

After the second fire, officials also changed the club's name to the Flossmoor Country Club. Since the railroad had established their Flossmoor station, uninitiated guests to the club easily became confused when their trains pulled into Homewood. Seeing a golf course on the right, many jumped off the train with their clubs in hand only to find the course adjacent to the Homewood station was the Ravisloe Country Club and not the Homewood course. Disheartened, the wayward golfers would either have to walk the 1-1/2 miles to the Homewood course or wait another hour or so for the next train. The 1914 name change certainly helped to alleviate this problem.

Ravisloe Country Club constructed this clubhouse in 1902. The club had previously used the home of Horace Briggs as its first clubhouse building. ***(Chicago Historical Society)***

The success of the Homewood Country Club spawned the development of other golf courses in the area. In the summer of 1901, another group of Chicago businessmen, this one led by Solomon Styx, initiated efforts to locate land to establish their own club. Styx had been bitten by the golf bug and convinced many of his colleagues, most of whom were members of the Standard Club of Chicago, to join him in pursuing this leisure pastime.

A Dutch farmer named Ravisloot owned the first parcel of interest they looked at. His property was located on 147th Street and was bisected by the Calumet River. It was initially thought that the river would serve as a recreational amenity for swimming and boating and that it would make a fine water hazard. The group soon found the water was too dirty for swimming, the river was prone to flooding, and the cost of building a bridge to support course maintenance equipment was too expensive. This site soon lost favor although prospective members continued to call the proposed club by the Ravisloot name. Some, however, thought the ending of the name too "guttural" and suggested changing to the softer sounding Ravislow or Ravisloe. The latter was agreed upon and eventually became the club's official name.

View of the pedestrian overpass the Illinois Central constructed in 1902 for the safety of Ravisloe Country Club members

View from the pedestrian overpass of the Illinois Central passenger depot (right) and their freight warehouse (left)

Another location being eyed, and the one finally selected, was the Sidney Briggs farm in Homewood. The farmstead proved to be just as attractive as the Ravisloot site. It was dotted with old elm and maple trees, which would provide an attractive appearance and much needed shade for the golfers. Much of the acreage was in pasture, which would allow the course to be developed with minimal effort and expense, and the farm was located just west of the Illinois Central tracks, which would allow members easy access from Chicago via I.C. suburban passenger trains. As the I.C. station was on the east side of the tracks, there was concern for the safety of members who would have to cross the tracks to walk to and from the course. This objection was overcome when the railroad agreed to construct a pedestrian overpass for the use of club members. In 1902, the railroad further enhanced service for golfers when it inaugurated a Golf Special, an express train that ran from the Randolph Street station downtown to Flossmoor, making stops at the country clubs along the way.

Negotiations with Mr. Briggs proved fruitful, and by August 1901, 101 acres of his farm were purchased with an option to buy additional land if needed. With this, Ravisloe Country Club became a reality, and members quickly set to work laying out the course and improving the grounds. Five holes were playable by the fall of 1901, and additional holes were developed in succeeding years until all eighteen holes were completed.

Louis Stumer's home was one of many summer homes built by affluent club members adjacent to the Ravisloe Country Club grounds.

A small cottage located on the course grounds served as the first clubhouse. The cottage was formerly the home of Mr. Briggs's parents, and being so small, it only afforded members a place to change and hang their clothing. For meals, members would bring their own picnic lunches, dine at the taverns in town, or visit an industrious farm family living near the club who sold chicken dinners for fifty cents apiece.

Construction of a larger wood frame clubhouse was completed in 1902. This clubhouse, located east of the present building, included a large great room with a brick fireplace, dining room, barroom, kitchen, and men's and women's locker rooms on the first floor. Seven rooms on the second floor were available for members to spend the night. These rooms lacked baths or clothes closets, so guests were limited to staying only a night. A large veranda extended across of the southern side of this building.

Early Ravisloe members included many famous names like Hart, Schaffner, Marx, Spiegel, and Julius Rosenwald, who would go on to become the president and CEO of Sears, Roebuck and Company. As was the case with the Homewood Country Club, some members built summer homes adjacent to the course, many of which still stand as a testament to a more genteel era. One of the largest homes was built by Louis Stumer on the west side of the course north of 183rd Street. Stumer, a successful Chicago milliner, owned five acres and built a large stucco mansion facing the course and decorated the interior with Italian marble finishes. Stumer spared no expense on the exterior landscaping either. In addition to a variety of ornamental shrubs, trees, and flowers planted on the estate, Stumer's property also included a swimming and boating pool measuring 150 feet long by 80 feet wide and 6 feet deep. The pool had a ten-foot by twenty-foot island in the center and was quite a novelty in the area. Stumer's home was torn down in 1973, and the homes on the Patricia Lane cul-de-sac occupy the site today.

Elaborate swimming and boating pool on the Stumer grounds *(Cowing Collection)*

The club flourished, and in 1910, a fifty-five-acre parcel was added to the course. With this addition, the course underwent a significant redesign, which was completed in 1913.

In the fall of that year, Ravisloe hosted an exhibition match between the English professionals Harry Vardon and Edward Ray and local amateurs "Chick" Evans and Warren Wood. Vardon and Ray complimented the course as being one of the best in the country and suggested a number of changes to make it even more challenging. The club hired renowned golf architect Donald Ross who implemented these and other changes in his redesign of the course completed between 1916 and 1920.

Construction started on Ravisloe's current clubhouse in 1916. This view shows the clubhouse, left, and the men's locker building, right.

About the time the initial course redesign was taking place, the club constructed a new men's locker room building. With the completion of this building, members realized the inadequacies of the main clubhouse, and plans were made to build a new one. Construction of a large Spanish Revival structure, the current clubhouse, was started in 1916 and, when completed, was one of the most luxurious in the country. New guest quarters were also constructed, and the second clubhouse building was moved on the grounds and refurbished into servants' quarters. Tennis courts and a swimming pool were added in subsequent years.

The club hired Robert White as its first professional in 1902. White, a native of St. Andrews, Scotland, was twenty-five when he took the job. Although an average golfer on the pro circuit, White excelled in course management. He studied agriculture during the winter months at the University of Wisconsin and became a pioneer in scientific turf grass management. He was

Advertisement for Robert White's P. G. Manufacturing Company *(Peter Georgiady)*

Bottom: **Members of Ravisloe's staff pose for this photo taken about 1910. Robert White, the club's first pro, is shown kneeling.** ***(Mae Everett)***

Idlewild Country Club's first clubhouse, which was completed in 1909 *(Idlewild Country Club)*

Elmer Farmer is shown driving the Idlewild Country Club's "station wagon," which transported members to and from the Illinois Central depot.

widely sought after to assist others in new course design and was regularly consulted on a myriad of issues relating to the successful growth of fairway turf and greens grasses. With this knowledge, White would go on to become a founding member of the American Society of Golf Course Architects.

An accomplished club maker, White also organized a cooperative of golf club makers named the P. G. Manufacturing Company in Homewood in 1908. At the time, club making was a "cottage industry," and the realm of family-owned concerns usually operated with very small staffs. Taking a cue from the British, White set up P. G. Manufacturing to spread business among a handful of local club makers to help smooth out the "boom and bust" cycles of production, so each shop could keep their hands occupied with regularity. P. G. Manufacturing facilities were located on the northwest corner of the intersection that today is known as Ridge Road and Park Avenue, west of the I.C. tracks. The company operated until 1914, the year White left Homewood for a job in New York.

Calumet Country Club's first clubhouse in Homewood was completed in 1917.

Calumet enlarged their clubhouse in 1921, and this is a view of the building from the course grounds.

White spent the formative years of his career at Ravisloe and gained a vast amount of valuable experience there. His peers certainly recognized his ability and elected him to serve as the first president of the Professional Golfers Association (PGA), which he helped organize in 1916.

At the same time White was organizing P. G. Manufacturing, a third golf course was established adjacent to Homewood. This course, located on acreage purchased from the Gottschalk family, had been the farmland of William and Henry Gottschalk and the land Benjamin Butterfield had originally homesteaded in 1838. This parcel was east of the Homewood Country Club and was bisected by Butterfield Creek. This club, known as the Idlewild Country Club, was incorporated on July 17, 1908, for the purpose of "pleasure and the promotion of outdoor sports and amusements." The first board of directors included Frederick Newman, president, and directors Martin Ascher, Frank Schornfeld, Henry Felsenthal, and Max Brandstetter. Each of the original members put up $25 earnest money to help get the club off the ground.

Al Naylor was engaged for a mere $60 per month to serve as the club's first professional. In this job, Naylor not only laid out the original course, he served as the head groundskeeper, taught the members the fine points of the game, ran the pro shop, and took charge of the caddy program. Naylor would hold the pro's job for over twenty-five years.

Construction on Idlewild's first clubhouse commenced in March 1909 and was completed later that year. The building was added onto over the years and was replaced by Idlewild's current clubhouse in 1965. Being a distance from the Flossmoor train station, the club ran a horse-drawn bus or "station wagon" to shuttle members to and from the depot during the golf season.

In the ensuing decades, two additional golf clubs opened in Homewood. Calumet Country Club moved to Homewood in 1917. Originally established in 1901, the club was located at Ninety-fifth Street and Cottage Grove Avenue on property now occupied by Chicago State University. "Pops" Tweedie laid out this course, which was close to the Illinois Central and only a half mile from Lake Calumet. By 1917, en-

A view of the front of Calumet's remodeled clubhouse in the late 1920s.

Advertisement for Klin Brothers Golf Clubs ***(Olympia Fields Country Club)***

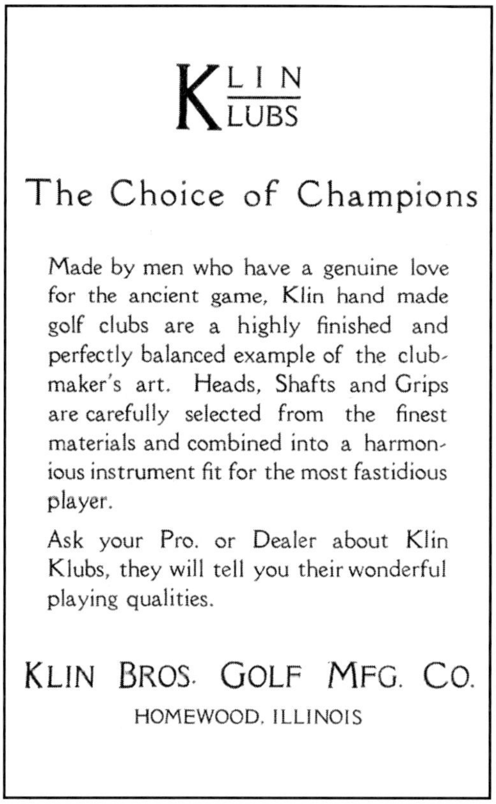

croaching industrialization convinced members to look for an alternate site. A 126-acre tract of land on 175th Street was bought from August Steiner in February 1917. Donald Ross was contracted to design the new course while club professional George Knox took charge of implementing Ross's plan. About the same time, Herman Stogentine was hired as the chief groundskeeper, a post he held for over forty years. A small one-room clubhouse was initially constructed, and this building was significantly added onto and remodeled in 1921. This same clubhouse, although extensively renovated over the years, still serves Calumet's members today.

The club was fortunate to have many Illinois Central executives listed among its members. This fact certainly did not hurt when the club petitioned for a stop of its own along the Illinois Central line. A station was established and has been known, then as now, as "Calumet." Calumet was also known for its dining offerings. Chef Charles Keiffer made a reputation for the club with the food he served at the Burnside location and continued that tradition in Homewood, preparing meals with only the freshest ingredients purchased from local farms.

Progress challenged the club again in 1956 when the Illinois Toll Authority announced plans for the Tri-State Tollway. Original plans called for only a small section of the course to be taken by the roadway. Despite reassurances to the contrary, the tollway took out a twenty-three-acre swath, which required a major renovation and produced the course members play on today.

Over the years, Calumet has played host to some of the world's greatest players. It was the site of the 1924 Western Open, won by Bill Mehlhorn; this was the first tournament to have scoring updates reported live by radio. Calumet also hosted the 1945 Chicago Victory Open. Byron Nelson won that tournament and left Calumet with his eighth straight PGA tournament win. Nelson would go on to win the next three tour events and rack up an amazing eleven consecutive tour

Klin Brothers also made golf clubs for children. ***(Olympia Fields Country Club)***

victories. His eighteen tournament wins for the 1945 season is a PGA tour record, and his scoring average that year of 68.33 was not surpassed until the 2000 season.

The last golf course established in Homewood, and the only one no longer in existence, was the Dixmoor Golf Club. Dixmoor was incorporated in October 1921, and Charles "Chick" Evans was listed as one of the club's first directors. By December 1921, the club had closed on the purchase of the 123-acre farm of Jabez Howe south of 175th Street, west of Dixie Highway, and directly across from the Calumet Country Club.

Dixmoor was organized as a semi-private club. Shares of stock were sold at $100 each, and those who purchased five or more shares were considered full members and entitled to all the privileges of the club. The general public was also welcome to use the course for a fee of $1 on weekdays and $2 on Sundays. The club built a large two-story frame clubhouse in the northeast section of its property, and its dining room was open to the public daily.

For some reason, Dixmoor was never a success and was closed in 1926, and the land was sold to a residential developer. The developer offered the clubhouse to the village for $5,000 although he estimated its value at over $50,000. An attractive deal, the proposition was put to a vote that village residents soundly rejected. The structure was later demolished, erasing any vestige of Dixmoor's existence.

With Dixmoor and the four country clubs operating in or next to Homewood, brothers Urban, Martin, and Eddie Klin found a fertile environment and started the Klin Brothers Golf Manufacturing Company to supply golf clubs to the burgeoning market in the Chicago area. In 1922, they rented the then vacant flourmill from the Steiner family and produced Klin *Drive Rite* brand clubs in Homewood until 1926 when they moved production facilities to Valparaiso, Indiana.

Although the names Klin Brothers, P. G. Manufacturing, and Dixmoor Golf Club are all forgotten relics of the past, golf and the survivors, Ravisloe, Idlewild, Calumet, and even the Flossmoor Country Club, have all been important parts of Homewood's history for over a century.

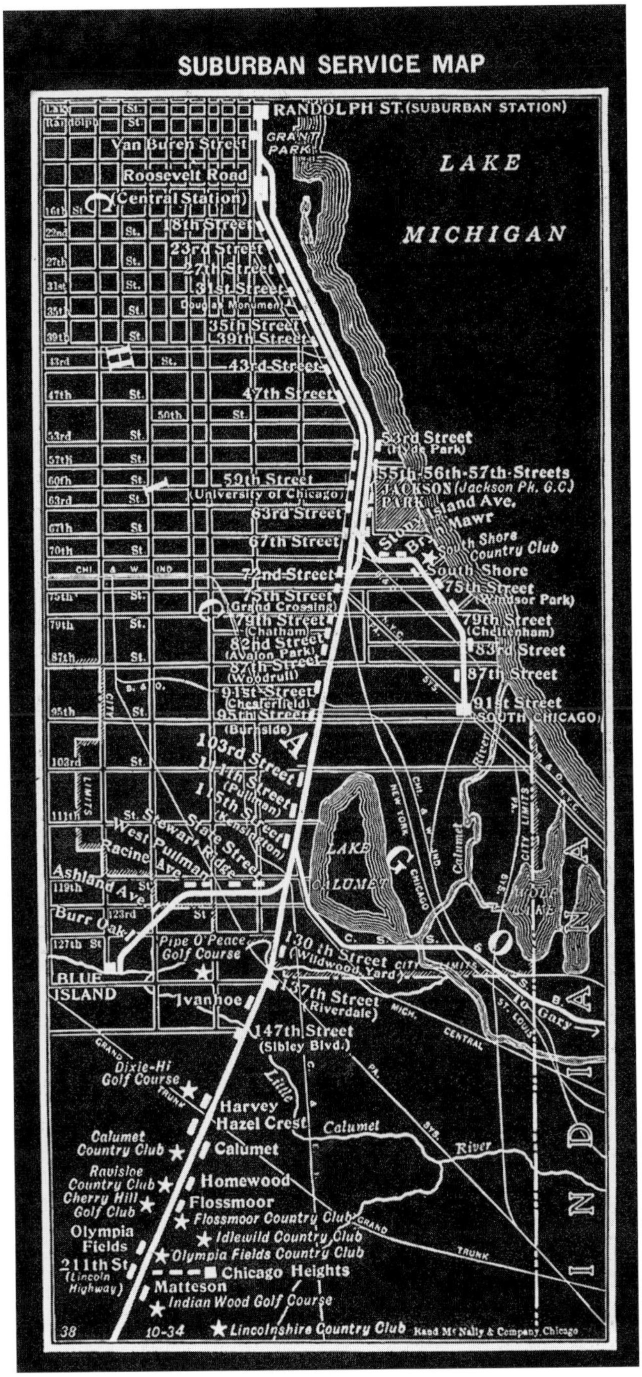

Map from 1934 shows the stops of the Illinois Central's Suburban Service, emphasizing the location of the numerous golf clubs near the train depots.

Members of Homewood's "Circle A's" baseball team

CHAPTER 8
Homewood Matures

While golf and the country club life were favorite pastimes of Chicago's elite, working class Homewoodians were content with enjoying more conventional and economical leisure activities. Memberships in fraternal organizations like the Modern Woodmen, the Independent Order of Odd Fellows, the Patriotic Order Sons of America, the Rebekah Lodge, and the Plattdeutche Gilde were popular after the turn of the century. These groups fostered community spirit by bringing members and families together for social, recreational, and service activities. Like the churches in town and the village's volunteer fire department, these fraternal organizations sponsored picnics in the summer months and many dinners and dances throughout the rest of the year. Another group, the Homewood Athletic Club, organized community baseball and football teams for the young men in the village. These teams, whose uniforms were emblazoned with the letter A centered in a circle, were known as the "Circle A's." The Circle A's competed with teams from communities throughout the surrounding area, many of whom were sponsored by local businesses. Homewood saloonkeeper William Brutlag sponsored another baseball team, the Brutlag Colts, whose members came from the "south end" of town.

Dances and elaborate invitations were hallmarks of Homewood's many fraternal organizations like the Modern Woodmen of America.

Ball games were always well attended, and team boosters took the train or horse and buggies to "away" games to cheer on their hometown sportsmen. In Homewood, the football field and a baseball diamond, complete

Homewood's baseball field was located east of the Chicago-Vincennes Road (Dixie Highway) and south of present-day Birch Road.

with spectators' bleachers, were located on land that was once a hayfield owned by Henry Gottschalk, east of the Chicago-Vincennes Road (Dixie Highway) around the present-day intersection of Birch Road.

Young and old alike also enjoyed sleighing parties in the winter and hayrides during the summer and fall months. By the teens, the increasing use of the automobile for commercial, agricultural, and recreational uses gave rise to the Sunday drive as an activity every member of the family looked forward to. More automobile traffic also led to demands by citizens for governments to provide better roads, which at this time consisted primarily of dirt and were passable in fair weather yet quickly became impassable mud holes after a few hours of rain. Better roads consisted of brick or macadam, which was crushed rock with a binder of tar or cement. These types of roads were generally found only in cities and towns and usually ended at the city limits. Motorists were clamoring for more improved roads of macadam and even concrete.

To address these demands, "good roads" movements sprang up in many areas throughout the country, and Homewood civic and business leaders recognized that improved roadways were the key to continuing growth and development in the village. The Homewood Good Roads Committee was formed in 1912 with the intent of raising funds to improve the roadways in the village and some of those leading into town. Within weeks of its organization, the committee had received pledges from residents and businesses totaling $3,000, well on the way to its goal of raising a total of $5,000.

By 1915, the good roads movement had gained significant momentum in the state of Illinois, and Homewood, being in close proximity to the city of Chicago, benefited by this. Chicago was the hub for many of the roads in the state, and three of the roads planned to be improved with state and county funds passed right through town. The Egyptian Trail, the Dixie Highway, and Halsted Street were all routes leading south of Chicago through Homewood, and these were paved with concrete between 1916 and 1920.

The Egyptian Trail was touted by the *Harvey Tribune* in its October 15, 1915, edition as being "a distinctive Illinois project in every way for one end is at Cairo, way down in Egypt, at the extreme southern end of the state and the other end is at Chicago, the metropolis of the state in the north. The building of this great road will do more to encourage the construction of good roads and to pull our fair state out of the mud than any other one thing that can be done." Exaggeration perhaps, but there was little question that the Egyptian Trail was in the vanguard of "modern" roadways that would span the length and breadth of Illinois.

The Egyptian Trail left Chicago via Halsted Street and traveled to Harvey where it turned southwest onto Park Avenue and traveled this route through Hazel Crest and Homewood. At Maria (183rd) Street in Homewood, the route proceeded west and then south on Matteson Road (Western Avenue). From Matteson, a number of existing roads were utilized to Peotone, Kankakee, and points farther south on the way to Cairo.

Sleighing parties were a popular winter pastime. This group is stopped in front of the old Salem Lutheran Church on Morris Avenue. ***(Mary Schoof)***

The Egyptian Trail, now Park Avenue, looking south from Pine Road *(Meyer Estate)*

At this early stage of auto travel, the state had few laws controlling signage or the flow of traffic. The Egyptian Trail Association, a consortium of communities the road passed through, set out rules governing road construction and uniform signage. Trail signs generally painted on telephone poles marked the route. The Egyptian Trail mark was a 12"x18" yellow sign painted on poles six feet from the ground. In the center of the sign, a black pyramid was painted flanked by the letter E on its left and the letter T on its right, both painted in black. These signs were painted at intervals and were meant to guide motorists along the way. Around Homewood, painter Joe Tienstra busied himself during the fall of 1915 and the spring of 1916 completing these pole markings. The association also called for the placement of signs marking dangerous curves, turns, intersections, and rail crossings. The signs were worded "Egyptian Trail-Danger-Sound Klaxon" and were placed three hundred feet ahead of any danger zone.

The Egyptian was well traveled during its heyday. The completion of the Governors Highway in the late 1920s, however, provided a more direct route between the Egyptian Trail communities, and today, few stretches of the Trail still carry its name.

The Dixie Highway was the brainchild of Carl Fisher, an Indianapolis native who was president of the Prest-O-Lite Battery Company, a founder of the Indianapolis Motor Speedway, and was credited with being the father of the Lincoln Highway, a transcontinental route connecting New York City with San Francisco that was started in 1913. Fisher envisioned a roadway linking Chicago with the yet undeveloped swamps of southeastern Florida now known as Miami Beach. It was no coincidence that Fisher owned large tracts of land in Florida and was interested in developing this acreage into a tourist mecca. Fisher enlisted the support of Midwestern and Southern governors who enthusiastically endorsed his proposal in April 1915. After this, plans for the first "interstate" highway linking north and south were quickly developed, and the route selected in Illinois followed the old Vincennes Trail, which was known as the Chicago-Vincennes Road in Homewood.

Survey work for the Dixie improvements in Homewood started in February 1916. This was followed by the installation of drain tile and culverts, and the first cement work converting the Vincennes Road to the new and improved Dixie Highway was started in October 1916 by the firm of Pronger and Fletcher of Blue Island. Paving in Homewood was completed by the end of July 1917.

The route the Dixie Highway followed in Illinois began at the intersection of Jackson Boulevard and Michigan Avenue in Chicago and proceeded south through Blue Island, Harvey, Homewood, and Chicago Heights, then followed what is Route 1 today through Crete, Beecher, Momence, Watseka, and down to Danville where the road turned east into Indiana. The route was marked by signage, which consisted of a white background with a wide band of red painted across the center on which the letters DH were painted in white.

Improvements to the balance of the highway in Illinois were completed by the summer of 1921. To mark this achievement, a motorcade took place on August 12 of that year. The motorcade, led by Illinois Governor Len Small, started in Danville and ended at the municipal

View of Dixie Highway looking north at the Main Street (Ridge Road) intersection

The second decade of the twentieth century witnessed a dramatic change in transportation. The horse and buggy was gradually replaced by the automobile as the vehicle of choice for recreational and commercial uses.

pier in Chicago. The day was declared Dixie Highway Day, and at each town the motorcade passed, groups of citizens in their own automobiles joined the procession. Mayor Fred Gold led the Homewood contingent to the ceremonies in Chicago that included speeches, a pageant, and a firemen's thrill show.

The third roadway to be improved through Homewood was Halsted Street. Billed as the longest street in any city in America, Halsted ran the length of the city of Chicago and by the end of 1917 had been completely paved with asphalt or concrete within the city limits. Chicago recognized the street's importance to commerce and industry and convinced Cook County officials to pave the road south of the city through the suburbs so that it could provide an improved link with the Lincoln Highway and help speed auto and truck traffic from the south and east into downtown Chicago. The paving was completed by the end of the decade, and Halsted Street has remained an important thoroughfare ever since.

Increased auto traffic also led to new problems in the village. Frequently, motorists using the Dixie Highway sped through town with little regard to the citizenry. Not only was this a danger to pedestrians crossing the street, the speeding autos and those without mufflers also spooked horses, which often led them to bolt in panic. Most times, the horses ran until they tired out or were reined in without causing any damage. Other times, the horses caused damage to the wagons or carriages they were hauling, and sometimes they even caused injuries to their drivers and to bystanders on the street. One particularly tragic example of this occurred on June 20, 1913, when a horse owned by butcher Henry Stolzenbach became frightened while on a delivery and began to run home. The horse, for unknown reasons, veered onto a sidewalk where Mrs. Fred Tatgenhorst and her son Earl and Mrs. Bert Goesel and her daughter Gertrude were walking. The adults were able to escape harm, but the children, who were walking a short distance ahead, were trampled under the horse's hooves. Young Earl recovered, but Gertrude, age five, died that day. More traffic also led to accidents between autos and horse and buggies and later between autos themselves.

Village trustees, heeding the many complaints made to them, took steps to control reckless driving in town. Speed limit signs were posted, and all automobiles were required to have mufflers. A four-way stoplight was placed in the center of the intersection of Main Street and the Dixie Highway in August 1917 to help prevent accidents there. By the end of the year, the wooden post for the light had been struck so many

View of Dixie Highway looking south from Main Street (Ridge Road). The village's first traffic signal is pictured in the center of the intersection.

times it had to be replaced, and the new light was mounted on a concrete base to prevent further damage. Curiously, a man named Howard Baxter of Kalamazoo, Michigan, even tried to recover $1,000 from the village for damages done to his car after he hit the post in October 1917. Rightfully, the village refused to pay.

As a further control measure, the village board approved the purchase of a police motorcycle and the hiring of William Huff as the first officer to operate it in March 1918. Homewood was now well equipped to deal with traffic violators, and as an incentive, the motorcycle officer was given $1 from the fines of every ticket he issued.

Unfortunately, it was a motorcycle officer who was Homewood's first and only police officer killed in the line of duty. On October 18, 1920, Homewood motorcycle officer Paul Edward Buckley joined state patrolman Earl Kessner chasing a car on the Dixie Highway. Kessner had observed the car break through a road construction barrier and initiated the chase. Buckley joined the chase in Homewood, and the two motor officers proceeded south on the Dixie Highway in hot pursuit of the traffic violator. As the chase neared "Al Sabbath's corner" (south of Holbrook Road), a delivery truck belonging to the Mandel Brothers Store of Chicago pulled across the highway. Overgrowth of trees and brush along the roadside obscured the motorcyclists' vision of the obstruction until it was too late. Buckley was unable to stop or swerve to avoid the truck and hit it broadside. Kessner, who was behind Buckley, swerved into a ditch and avoided any injury. The offender's vehicle escaped unscathed.

Buckley was taken to St. James Hospital by a passing automobile and was initially thought not to be severely injured. He was conscious after the accident and appeared to be slightly bruised about the head. Looks were deceiving. Buckley suffered internal injuries and died the next morning.

To compound the tragedy, village employees were not insured at the time. Donations were collected for Buckley's burial expenses and to help his widow and three young children. After his burial was paid for, excess funds in the amount of $265.10 were given to Mrs. Buckley. As is the case so many times, the village board passed a motion after the accident to provide accident and liability insurance coverage on the village's police officers and workmen, too late to be of any help to the Buckley family.

The growing use of the automobile also led to new businesses opening in town. The old blacksmith and wagon shops and the men who operated them were not as proficient in servicing and repairing the "newfangled" automobiles. As the horse and buggy days waned, the era of the auto repair garage and service station dawned. In Homewood, the first auto repair garage, the Homewood Garage and Livery, opened on Morris Avenue (Harwood Avenue) north of Main Street in March 1912. The Hawkins brothers who owned the business not only repaired cars, they sold used vehicles, had cars for rent, and being close to the railroad depot, also operated an express package and delivery service. Over ninety years later, a repair garage in a newer building is still located at this site (18009 Harwood Avenue).

In 1915, Andrew Severson opened his repair garage in a small frame building on the southwest corner of the current intersection of Dixie Highway and Elm Road. Business was good from the start, so Severson built a larger cement block structure on the site to house the repair garage and a gasoline station in 1916. A few years later, operation of Severson's Garage was taken over by his son-in-law Ted Utermark Sr. The garage building was demolished in 1966, and the property is now site of the Homewood fire station.

The former First Presbyterian Church was moved to the southwest corner of Dixie Highway and Elm Road in 1915. Andrew Severson opened his auto repair garage in this building that same year.

Auto repair garages were not the only shops opening in Homewood's expanding business district. Henry Funk had a large two-story brick building built next to his grocery store on Main Street in 1911. The first floor of the

Severson's second garage building was erected on the corner of Dixie Highway and Elm Road. The business was later taken over by Theodore Utermark. *(Meyer Estate)*

Main Street (Ridge Road) looking east from Harwood Avenue. Sachs' Drug Store and the Homewood Theatre are visible on the right. Egan's Barber Shop and the Homewood Post Office are in the first building on the left.

building contained space for two storefronts while the second floor contained a large open hall where various community groups held meetings, dances, dinners, and other functions. For years, the building was known as Funk's Hall and still stands with a renovated façade at 2049-51 Ridge Road. On the first floor of Funk's building, druggist Jacob Sachs opened the Homewood Drug Company, which was the first business in town to have an electric sign hanging on its exterior. In the other half on the first floor, Jacob and Fannie Schwab established the People's Store where they sold dry goods and clothing. Upstairs, John Hruby rented the hall on Monday and Thursday evenings to show moving pictures. The first film shown was the two-part epic "The Life of Moses." The moving picture shows were a big hit in town, and by the end of 1911, Hruby was also showing films on Saturday nights.

By the early teens, Homewood's business district had expanded to such an extent that many merchants had an opportunity to move to larger or more prime locations. Then, as now, businesses frequently moved to take advantage of better storefronts to improve their sales, and many times, a business moved more than once during its lifespan.

In 1912, Henry Gottschalk completed an addition to the east end of the Homewood State Bank building, and Arthur Farr moved his dry goods and clothing store into this space (2023 Ridge Road) from the smaller store he had operated on Martin Avenue. In the space Farr vacated, Henry Puhrmann opened a grocery store in 1914. Puhrmann later partnered with his brother-in-law Edward Lange, and the pair moved their store onto Main Street into the storefront formerly occupied by Henry Funk's grocery. The Farr Mercantile Company went bankrupt in 1915, and following that, the Schwabs' People's Store moved from the Funk's Hall building down the street into the bank addition. The Homewood Theatre then moved into the space the Schwabs vacated. By this time, Henry and Amelia Brockman were operating the theatre, and Amelia was playing the piano as an accompaniment to heighten the drama of the silent movies.

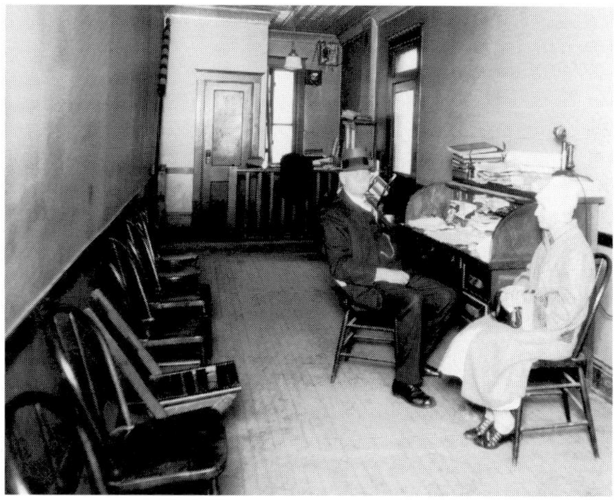

To make room for the addition to the bank building, Henry Gottschalk had his father's house moved several lots east on the south side of Main Street. After William Gottschalk died in 1903, Henry assumed ownership of the home. Once moved, a 24' addition was built onto the front of the building, and it was completely veneered with brick. Renovations to the building were completed in May 1912 after which Oscar Robertson opened the New England Hotel and Restaurant in it. The hotel boasted "24 rooms, with steam heat and all other modern improvements." The old place had come full circle and returned to its original use as a hotel.

Judge J. C. Howe inside his office on Main Street (Ridge Road) ***(Cowing Collection)***

Early view of St. Joseph's Church, built in 1912, on the Chicago-Vincennes Road (Dixie Highway)

Homewood's expanding business district was an outgrowth of the village's increasing popularity as a residential community. In 1911 alone, thirty-four new houses were built in town, and home building continued unabated throughout much of the rest of the decade. By 1920, Homewood's population had grown to 1,389. In addition to Frank Riedle, Jabez Howe Jr. was also engaged in real estate sales in the village and had a small office on Main Street east of Funk's Hall.

The second First Presbyterian Church was completed in 1915 on Gottschalk Avenue.

Howe would later move his office across the street to the north side of Main Street. A practicing attorney, Howe was elected to serve as the village's police magistrate or justice of the peace from 1903 through 1931. To most residents, he was known as Judge Howe. James Cowing, Fred Gold, and James Akhurst were other realtors selling homes during the latter part of the decade.

With a growing population, Homewood's religious denominations grew also. In January 1912, the village board approved a request from Father Armand Martin to use the meeting room of the village hall on Sunday mornings. After January 14, Mass was celebrated there for the area's Roman Catholics. In May, the Archdiocese of Chicago purchased a lot storekeeper Henry Zimmer owned on the east side of the Chicago-Vincennes Road across from the village hall. Ground was broken for a frame church in June, and by the end of the year, the church building was completed and consecrated to Saint Joseph. Father Martin was succeeded by Father John Doran who was appointed the first pastor of St. Joseph's Church in 1914. One of Father Doran's first acts was to baptize Helena, Gratia, and Clarence Joseph Trappe, children of C. J. Trappe, the village's electrician and owner of a store selling electrical appliances. For years, the organist at St. Joseph's was Lucy Grannis, who later married Henry Puhrmann.

By 1914, the old church building east of the railroad tracks in which the Presbyterians had been holding services was no longer large enough for their growing congregation. Property was purchased north of the George Kern home on Gottschalk Avenue, and the cornerstone for a new frame church was laid on November 7. Once the new building was completed in 1915, the old church was sold to Andrew Sever-

The original First Presbyterian Church building had a long history. First a church, then an auto repair garage, the building was later enlarged to make this apartment house which stood on Dixie Highway, between Elm and Chestnut, for about fifty years. ***(William F. Moore)***

son, who moved the structure a block to the south and converted it into his first auto repair garage and then into a two-story apartment building. After fifty years as an apartment house, the old church was burned down in 1966 to make room for the garage section of the Homewood fire station on Dixie Highway.

Not to be outdone, the members of St. Paul Church also enlarged their building in 1915. The structure was raised three feet off the ground, and a basement was built underneath. While this work was underway, the rear of the sanctuary was lengthened by sixteen feet. Much of this work was done by members of the congregation and was completed by the time the church celebrated its fiftieth anniversary on October 24, 1915.

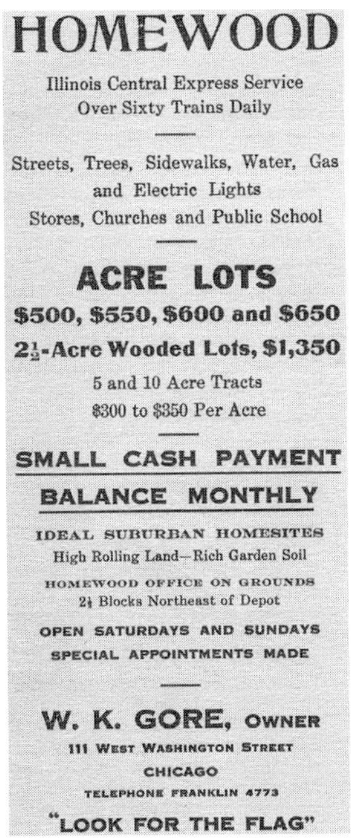

W. K. Gore was one of many real estate developers promoting Homewood during the decade. Gore developed lots on Pine, Cedar, and Maple Roads east of the Illinois Central tracks. ***(Cowing Collection)***

Four years later, Homewood Lutherans officially established their congregation. Although Lutherans had been meeting in private homes and the village hall under the auspices of Reverend Matthew Fedderson of St. John's Church in Coopers Grove (Country Club Hills) since Christmas 1905, a church was not organized until August 1919. The congregation was affiliated with the Missouri

Monument for Homewood's World War I dead. Initially installed on the northeast corner of Main Street (Ridge Road) and the Dixie Highway, the boulder was later moved to a park next to the village library. It now rests in the Veterans Memorial Park on Harwood Avenue at Olive Road.

Synod on September 14, and Salem was the name chosen by the membership for their church. Original members included William Adam, Henry Butze, Walter Gommoll, John Kaehler, William Kaehler, Christ Ratschlag, Herman Stogentine, Albert Tatge, Charles Harmke, and Henry and John Fiebig.

After organizing, the congregation purchased two twenty-five-foot lots on Morris Avenue south of 183rd Street from member Henry Butze, and a carpenter shop located on the property was remodeled into an attractive sixteen-foot by twenty-six-foot church. Salem's first house of worship was dedicated on November 9, 1919. This building was used until a new and larger church built by members John Kaehler and Henry Butze was erected in 1925.

A fifth denomination, the Christian Scientists, met in space on the second floor of the Homewood State Bank building throughout much of the decade. Members of this congregation later merged with the Christian Science Church in Chicago Heights.

On a national level, the teens were notable for major events that affected the lives of those in Homewood also. Women were given the right to vote, the world went to war, and a flu epidemic ravaged the nation killing over 600,000 Americans.

After the turn of the twentieth century, the women's suffrage movement gained significant headway. In Illinois, suffrage groups lobbied the state legislature intensively on the issue of allowing women the right to vote. These efforts proved fruitful when, in June 1913, the Illinois House and Senate both passed bills giving women this right. Illinois was the first state east of the Mississippi to do so, and women in the state responded by turning out in force on election day.

The municipal elections of April 1914 were the first elections in which women could vote. In Homewood, out of a total of 392 votes cast in this election, 159 were cast by women. Ice cream and candy shop owner Clara Nieburger held the distinction as being the first woman to cast a vote in the Homewood election. It wasn't until August 1920 that the Nineteenth Amendment to the United States Constitution took effect, allowing women across the country the right to vote in all elections.

Nieburger, unfortunately, would figure prominently in another main event of the decade—the Spanish Influenza Epidemic of 1918. The epidemic, which started unknowingly in March on an army installation in Kansas, spread with great speed. Public health officials were helpless to control it. They distributed masks, closed schools, and forbade large indoor public assemblies, but nothing seemed to help. Over the course of nine months, the death toll was enormous. In October alone, 195,000 Americans succumbed to the flu. By the end of November, the number of deaths began to plunge, and the epidemic faded away as inexplicably as it started.

Nieburger died of the flu in October, and she was one of a number of victims in Homewood. Other victims included Henry Stolzenbach Jr., sisters Alvina Dahlmann and Josephine Meyer, and Andrew Chellar and William Nuessle, who both contracted the flu while serving in the U.S. Army.

At the time of the epidemic, America was a nation at war. Draft call-ups, bond drives, and troop shipments were all in high gear, and these certainly may have helped to exacerbate the flu's spread. The Great War, ultimately known as World War I, had been raging in Europe since July 1914. The war pitted Germany and Austria-Hungary against France, the United Kingdom, and Russia and subsequently involved many more nations.

This was an uneasy time in Homewood as many residents were German immigrants and still had family in Germany. Some even secretly supported the "Kaiser." The United States tried to remain neutral, but the sinking of the British passenger liner *Lusitania* and similar aggression by German U-boats against American ships changed public opinion. President Woodrow Wilson signed a joint resolution of Congress declaring a state of war between the United States and Germany on April 6, 1917. In May, the Selective Service Act was passed requiring all young men between the ages of twenty-one and thirty-one to register for the "draft." The draft increased the size of the armed forces from 200,000 people to almost four million by the end of the war.

The first Homewood men drafted left town for service in September 1917. The village's volunteer firefighters held a farewell party for these "boys" on September 15 at Funk's Hall, and the soon-to-be soldiers were feted with dinner, a few speeches, and a "goodly amount of smokes" to take with them. Eventually, sixty-four Homewood men served with the American Expeditionary Forces, and all but four returned home safely. In addition to flu victims Chellar and Nuessle, Edward D. Haigh died of disease also. Sadly, Haigh contracted diphtheria in France after the war had ended but before his unit was shipped home. He died April 18, 1919. The only Homewood serviceman to die in combat was Alfred Wolland. Wolland enlisted with the Royal Artillery, Canadian Expeditionary Forces, soon after the outbreak of hostilities in 1914. Little else is known about Wolland and his military service except that his battalion was completely wiped out in battle in 1916.

Nineteen months after the United States entered the war, it ended. Armistice occurred at the eleventh hour on the eleventh day of the eleventh month 1918. Word of the armistice reached Homewood about 3:00 A.M. central time. Shortly afterwards, resident Thomas Weiss climbed the belfry of St. Paul Church to ring the bell. The whistles of nearby Illinois Central steam locomotives also began to blow. People all over town were jarred awake by this commotion, which continued incessantly. As many ran outside of their homes, they heard the words, "the war is over!" re-echo down the streets of Homewood. The joy was contagious. People shouted until they were hoarse and banged pots and pans while marching in an impromptu parade, which ended at Louis Mueller's tavern where the Kaiser was hung in effigy. Later, many Homewood residents attended services at the community's churches giving thanks this tribulation had passed.

James Kentish, holding the flag, leads other World War I veterans in a parade past the old Homewood Village Hall.

By the fall of 1919, all of Homewood's servicemen had returned home, and Village President Fred Gold organized a "Welcome Home" committee to plan a suitable celebration. A banquet was held at the Presbyterian Church for all who served in the war, and many of the men present expressed the desire to form a veterans' organization. As an outgrowth of this event, Homewood Post 483 of the American Legion was established on December 15, 1919, with twenty-two veterans signing as charter members. Victor Armitage was elected the post's first commander.

As the decade drew to a close, the world was finally at peace, and the residents of Homewood looked forward to a prosperous future.

Julius Andresen stands behind a relatively barren bar in his tavern. It is likely this picture was taken just after the start of Prohibition in 1920. Andresen later sold the place to Ernie Sanders.

CHAPTER 9

The Roaring Twenties

After World War I ended, the United States rose to the rank of a world power. While European nations struggled to recover from the ravages of war, the United States benefited from overseas territories, a plentiful supply of raw materials, and access to new markets abroad. Assembly line production increased, which led to lower prices and encouraged mass consumption. The country's economy soared throughout the rest of the following decade, earning the period the title—the Roaring Twenties. Homewood, too, shared in this prosperity: new businesses opened, home building increased, and the village's population more than doubled to 3,227 by decade's end.

The 1920s was also a decade of contradiction. Conservative interests had fought for years to outlaw the sale and consumption of intoxicating liquors to help curb crime and the incidences of public drunkenness. The Anti-Saloon League of America succeeded in these efforts when the Eighteenth Amendment to the United States Constitution, known as the National Prohibition Act, took effect on January 16, 1920. The manufacture, sale, and consumption of all beverages with an alcohol content of more than 0.5% was now illegal. Unpopular, Prohibition had somewhat of an opposite effect and spawned a wave of organized criminal activity where the terms bootlegger, speakeasy, and gangster became a part of the nation's parlance.

In Homewood, the concept of Prohibition was never popular. As early as 1914, residents expressed their opinions in an advisory referendum with 117 "dry" votes cast in favor and 221 "wets" cast opposed to outlawing liquor. At the time Prohibition took effect in 1920, four taverns were operating in the village. On the southwest corner of the Dixie

Highway and Main Street, Ed Billings was operating the old Lehmke tavern that Gustave Beck had operated for about ten years before. A short time later, Billings closed shop, and Frank Kaja leased the building where he opened a barbeque restaurant. Farther west on the southeast corner of Main Street and Morris (Harwood) Avenue, Julius Andresen was running the tavern and rooming house across the street from the Illinois Central depot. Through the teens, this tavern had been run by a number of people including John Schultz, Henry Krumm, and Charles Wenzel. By 1923, Ernie Sanders took over this business and made a name for himself selling his famous chicken dinners, near beer, and soft drinks. Across the road, on the north side of Main Street, Louis Mueller Sr. "retired" from tavern keeping and rented the first floor of his building to Joseph Mandernack who operated a soft drink parlor there. Mueller, however, continued to live on the second floor. Finally, on the south side of town, Mrs. Sophie Brutlag closed her tavern, and Earl Multog later opened a candy, ice cream, and soda shop in the space the Brutlag tavern vacated.

By the mid-1920s, the criminal element had capitalized on the sale of illegal beverages. Bootleggers set up their own breweries and distilleries and sold the beer and whiskey they made to illegal saloons or "speakeasies" often set up in the back rooms and basements of legitimate businesses. Fierce competition between bootlegging gangs resulted, which frequently erupted into gun battles over territory. In the south suburbs, famed Chicago mobster Al Capone controlled much of this illegal activity. At times, he was forced to fend off challenges to his "turf" by rivals, some of whom came from Chicago Heights.

Homewood did not escape the effects of this turf warfare. Two notable incidents occurred during 1926. One involved the bombing on May 15 of the Amalfi Gardens, a restaurant at 175th Street and the Dixie Highway popular for fine dining, dancing, and perhaps a little "liquid refreshment." John Vallortigara opened the roadhouse a year before and had established a steady trade and loyal clientele. After the bombing, which caused about $5,000 damage to the building, Vallortigara could only speculate "competitors" were responsible. Whoever was to blame, Vallortigara may have heeded the message they were trying to send, as he had no other problems at the restaurant for the remaining ten years he owned it. After that, a number of people ran the restaurant until the Surma brothers took over in 1946.

Two and a half weeks after the Amalfi bombing, the "booze war," as the *Chicago Tribune* called it, hit close to home with fatal results.

Early June 2, Phillip Piazza, a gang boss from Chicago Heights and a former Capone associate, and his lieutenant, Jimmie Lamberta, were entertaining two women at the Derby Inn. The Derby Inn was a roadhouse located on the southeast corner of 175th and Halsted Streets, which at the time was in an unincorporated area east of town. Piazza, who had recently taken over the lease to the building, was in the process of remodeling it, and the two couples had gone there about midnight to inspect the progress. Shortly after 1:00 A.M., the couples left the inn and were ambushed by "shotgun assassins" who were lying in wait in a cornfield adjacent to the building. Lamberta and one of the women were killed by the shotgun blasts as they walked to their car. Piazza and the other woman escaped unharmed. Later that morning, the bullet-riddled car was towed to Severson's Garage in Homewood, causing quite a stir amongst townspeople.

Police had no question these murders were alcohol-related, given Piazza's poor relationship with Capone and the fact his business in Chicago Heights had been raided a year before and was found to harbor one of the largest stills in south Cook County. Piazza's luck, however, did not last long. He was gunned down a month later on July 22 at the Milano Café, the business he owned in Chicago Heights.

The Illinois Kennel Club's dog-racing track, built in 1926, was located on the southeast corner of Halsted and 175th Streets. The Menard's Home Improvement store occupies the site today. ***(Chicago Historical Society)***

The Derby Inn gave promise of much patronage. It was located next to the greyhound racetrack of the Illinois Kennel Club and across the street from the Washington Park Race Track. Both tracks held their inaugural races on July 3, 1926.

The dog track was built and operated by a group led by J. Homer Ellis and A. L. Spindler, both of Chicago Heights, Jack Chambers of Memphis, and George Parton, who was also secretary of the Tampa Kennel Club in Florida. The track was a 5/16ths-mile oval rather than the standard 1/4-mile dog-racing track. In addition to the grandstand and paddock areas, the track had kennel facilities for over three hundred greyhounds and was lighted by several half-million candlepower floodlights. A larger racetrack on which auto and motorcycle races were held surrounded the dog-racing oval. The dog track, later known as the Thornton Coursing Club, ceased operation in 1934 likely due to the effects of the Depression and ongoing legal problems related to gambling issues.

A groom and a trainer show some of the dogs that raced at the Illinois Kennel Club's track on Halsted Street. ***(Chicago Historical Society)***

On the west side of Halsted Street, the Washington Park Corporation and the Illinois Jockey Club built the Washington Park Race Track. Construction on the facility started in the spring of 1924. Situated on 206 acres south of 175th Street, Washington Park boasted a massive steel and concrete grandstand, a clubhouse, judges stand, and paddock area. Thirty stables capable of accommodating over one thousand horses were also constructed. Every effort was made to transform the former prairie land into a "floral gem." Special grass seed was sown on the infield, and ornamental shrubbery and flowering plants were placed throughout the facility. To complete the park-like setting, fifteen- to twenty-year-old elm trees were transplanted from Wisconsin to grace the boulevard entrances to the track grounds.

During the early years, Washington Park played host to the revival of the American Derby, dubbed the "greatest racing classic in the Western Hemisphere." Later, on August 31, 1955, record crowds saw the most famous match in U.S. thoroughbred history between Swaps and Nashua at Washington Park. Swaps had beaten Nashua in the Kentucky Derby, but Nashua won the Belmont and the Preakness Stakes that year. Since both horses held partial claim to the Triple Crown, a match race was held. Swaps was the favorite, but Nashua, jockeyed by Eddie Arcaro, won by 6-1/2 lengths. The race was broadcast live to an estimated fifty million viewers by CBS Television.

Washington Park was a fixture in Homewood for over fifty years. The end came suddenly on a bitterly cold night in 1977. The track had been hosting its first winter season of harness racing, and on February 5, fire was discovered in the grandstand. Within hours, the grandstand and clubhouse building was reduced to a pile of twisted steel and smoldering ashes, forever ending the reign of the "sport of kings" in Homewood.

At the same time the racetracks were opening for business, the Illinois Central Railroad was completing construction on two major projects. One, the construction of the Markham Yards, changed the landscape of northeast Homewood permanently. The yards, named after Charles Markham, the railroad's president at the time, were the Illinois Central's massive freight classification yards built between 157th Street in Harvey on the north and Pine Road in Homewood on the south. The yards, initially proposed in the fall of 1917, were meant to consolidate the transfer and switching of the I.C.'s freight car traffic

View of the grandstand and grounds of the Washington Park Race Track, completed in 1926, located on the southwest corner of Halsted and 175th Streets.

Nashua working out for his famous match race against Swaps held on August 31, 1955, at Washington Park

Washington Park Race Track Program

in and out of Chicago. Included as part of this project was an extensive complex of mechanical and repair facilities to help maintain the railroad's fleet of steam locomotives and freight cars. A roundhouse, coaling tower, and machine and boiler shops were among the buildings built on the west side of Ashland Avenue north of Maple Road.

Prior to the start of construction, the railroad had to negotiate the purchase of up to 650 acres of land in the city of Harvey and the villages of Homewood, East Hazel Crest, and Hazel Crest. In Homewood, some homes and outbuildings were either torn down or moved. Sections of the Dixie Highway and Maple, Cedar, and Pine Roads were also vacated to allow construction to proceed.

Land north of Ridge Road, now a part of the Izaak Walton Preserve, showing the rolling hills where sand was taken and used as fill by the Illinois Central ***(Jean Mackenzie)***

Steam shovel excavating sand on the Mackenzie farm for use as fill by the Illinois Central ***(Jean Mackenzie)***

Initial work on the project started in 1918 and consisted of the movement of a part of the five million cubic yards of sand used as fill needed to level swampy areas and elevate track. One and a half million cubic yards of this sand came from the Mackenzie farm, the area north of Ridge Road now a part of the land and lakes of the Izaak Walton Preserve. These sand deposits also provided ample evidence of the area's geologic past as part of the ancient shoreline of Lake Michigan. Construction of the yards slowed significantly after President Wilson signed the Railway Control Act in March 1918. The act federalized the nation's railroads during the war for troop and material shipments. Work did not resume on the yard project until 1922. The Dixie Highway subway (viaduct) was completed that year, and the remainder of the construction was finished in 1926. Markham Yards were officially opened on April 1.

Elimination of all grade crossings between downtown Chicago and Richton was a goal of the railroad as part of the I.C.'s electrification of its suburban or commuter services, the second major project it undertook during the 1920s. The

Aerial view of the Illinois Central's roundhouse and Markham Yards is taken looking west over Ashland Avenue. The Dixmoor Golf Club can be seen in the distance in the upper right of the photo. ***(Illinois Central Historical Society)***

growing population along the rail line and the increasing use of the automobile led to more fatal accidents at these crossings. Prior to the construction of the viaduct, the Dixie Highway crossed the rail tracks at grade on an angle near the Maple Road intersection. Fatal accidents there had become quite numerous, earning the intersection the apt name of "death's angle." In 1919 alone, eight people were killed at the crossing despite the fact a flagman was usually stationed there to stop traffic when trains approached. Five of those killed that year died in a New Year's Eve accident when their car was struck by a southbound freight train and was then hit a second time by a northbound passenger train. Fortunately, the construction of the Maria (183rd) Street and the Flossmoor Road viaducts were completed in 1913, and the pedestrian subway at Main Street (Ridge Road) in Homewood was built in 1911, which no doubt eliminated further fatal accidents at these locations.

The electrification of the I.C.'s suburban trains was a great benefit to Homewood and all the communities the trains passed through. Not only were the trains more efficient and dependable, but also they no longer required a steam engine for motive power. This eliminated the smoke that commuter steam engines generated each day on the many trips they made to and from downtown Chicago. A real nuisance, the smoke and hot ash fouled the air, set off occasional prairie fires, and left a film of soot and grime on anything they touched. The area wouldn't be completely free of this nuisance until 1957 when the last steam freight locomotive was retired from service on the Illinois Central.

Construction of the steel supports for the electrification wiring started in Homewood in October 1925. By July 1926, track modifications had been made, new train cars had been delivered, and the electrification project was completed. Formal dedication ceremonies were held on August 7 and included the arrival in Chicago of four Official Electrification Specials, one originating at Matteson and the others at Blue Island, South Chicago, and Forty-seventh Street. After their arrival at the I.C.'s Central Station, a grand parade with over four hundred floats took place, which ended at the recently completed Soldier Field. At Soldier Field, a Pageant of Transportation, featuring historic and modern equipment of the Illinois Central Railroad, was held, and the day's events were capped off with a banquet for over twelve hundred guests held at the Palmer House Hotel.

Aerial view of an Illinois Central train traveling north out of Homewood. Dixie Highway is visible at right, and the photo shows how the road crossed the tracks at an angle and on grade near Maple Avenue.

Death's Angle, the notoriously dangerous grade crossing of the Dixie Highway on the Illinois Central tracks, is barely visible at the right in this photo. North of the crossing, Dixie Highway traveled on the west side of the rail tracks as it does today. ***(Illinois Central Historical Society)***

Homewood residents participated with gusto in the dedication ceremonies. Crowds gathered along the tracks to cheer the Electrification Special on its way downtown from Matteson. The depot was festooned with flags and flowers, and Homewood officials, led by Village President John Seator, Henry Gottschalk, Frank Prindiville, and Frank Cowing, boarded the Electrification Special as it stopped in Homewood. Homewood also sent three floats to participate in the Electrification Parade, and Ruth Wildman rode one of the floats as "Miss Homewood." A grand time was had by all who participated.

A special feature at the Palmer House banquet was a large painting of Homewood's new depot displayed as a backdrop to the speaker's table. The Spanish Mission-style depot, built to complement the Ravisloe clubhouse, was completed at the end of 1923 and was located on the west side of the tracks. The building still serves as Amtrak's passenger station in Homewood. After completion of this new building, the Illinois Central donated the old frame depot, built some seventy years before, to the Homewood Women's Club.

One of the floats Homewood sent to the Illinois Central's Electrification Parade in 1926 pauses in front of Lorado Taft's sculpture "A Fountain of Time" in Chicago.

The Women's Club, organized in 1920, had been using a room in the home of Fred and Eliza Gold to store and exchange books collected by members. As time went on, the collection grew, and the idea of a public library was born. The women lobbied for the old rail depot, and funds were raised to move it to a site the village owned called Triangle Park. The park, located east of the rail tracks and north of the corner of Harwood Avenue and the Dixie Highway, was also the site of a memorial dedicated to the World War I veterans who died in service. The depot was moved to this location in March 1924 and after remodeling was ready for use by the fall of that year. The Women's Club raised money to support the library by publishing a newspaper for the village in cooperation with the Homewood Chamber of Commerce. The first issue of this weekly paper, called the *Homewood News*, was printed on November 29, 1924, and early editors included Virgil Smith,

The Dixie Highway viaduct nearing completion in October 1922 ***(Bob and Barb Harms)***

Eleanor Howe, who would later earn fame as a Chicago radio hostess, and Paul Martin. The paper was purchased by the Williams Press in Chicago Heights in 1932 and was then published as a section of the *Chicago Heights Star* for a number of years until the *Homewood-Flossmoor Star* became a separate edition. In April 1927, after voter approval, the library became a tax-supported institution under control of an elected board of trustees.

Illinois Central completed construction of this Spanish Mission-style depot on the west side of the tracks in 1923. The design was meant to mimic the Ravisloe clubhouse.

The Illinois Central depot was just one of a number of new commercial buildings built in Homewood during the decade. Two of the structures built housed banks, which served as a further testament to the prosperity of Homewood residents. A new bank, the Cook County Trust and Savings Bank, opened for business on January 10, 1925, in a brick building built on the southwest corner of the Dixie Highway and Main Street. This building replaced the old frame tavern building that had stood on the corner for almost seventy years. The old tavern building was moved a lot to the south and continued to serve as a Homewood landmark and tavern until it burned down in 1957. The bank was capitalized with $50,000 in stock, and James Cowing was the bank's first president, Dr. William Doepp II was vice president, and George Thies was the bank's first cashier.

Parking at the train station has always been a problem as this early view suggests. *(Meyer Estate)*

The Illinois Central's old frame depot was moved to a triangular piece of land just east of the Dixie Highway viaduct and converted into Homewood's public library in 1924.

Not to be outdone, the Homewood State Bank moved into new quarters in April 1925. The State Bank, which had operated out of a building on the southeast corner of Main Street and Martin Avenue, built larger facilities on the northwest corner of the same intersection. At the time of the move, Henry Gottschalk, the bank's first president, was still serving in that capacity, a post he had held since 1908.

A third financial institution operating in the village was the Homewood Building and Loan Association. Established in July 1920, the Association was organized by local residents and business owners interested in having people own their own homes. Henry Gottschalk, James Cowing, and Village President Fred Gold were some of the founders of this institution, which started with subscribed capital of $69,500. The Building and Loan, later known as the Homewood Savings and Loan Association, had office space in the Homewood State Bank building.

At the time the Building and Loan was opening, Fred Gold was also starting the Homewood Coal, Ice and Material Company in the ice yard he had purchased from Ed Bang on 183rd Street west of the I.C. tracks. In addition to continuing to harvest and sell ice, Gold also began to sell coal and a complete line of building materials. On the east side of the tracks, a couple of blocks south of 183rd Street, Henry Fiebig opened the Guaranteed Fuel and Supply Company. Fiebig also

The Cook County Trust & Savings Bank, the Homewood Post Office and Cowing Realty building and the Homewood Hotel are pictured in this mid-1920s view of the south side of Main Street (Ridge Road). *(Cowing Collection)*

The Homewood State Bank built this building on the northeast corner of Main Street (Ridge Road) and Martin Avenue in 1925. This view is looking west on Main Street (Ridge Road) from Martin Avenue. *(Great Lakes Bank)*

sold coal and building materials and harvested ice from another pond Ed Bang had near this location. Competing with Gold and Fiebig to supply the demands of the burgeoning construction trade in Homewood was the Chicago and Riverdale lumberyard located next to the old Steiner mill.

Fred Gold was also involved in real estate sales and development. In 1924, Gold helped broker the sale of the George Mertens homestead located on the northeast corner of the Dixie Highway and Main Street. After the sale was completed, the house was moved a lot to the east, and construction started on the two-story "Homewood" Building on the corner lot. The Homewood Building, built with beautiful white terra cotta brick, was completed in May 1925. The Community Pharmacy, owned and operated by

druggist Walter Muszynski, was the main tenant of the building; other first tenants included the Homewood Cleaners, the Consumer's Sanitary Coffee and Butter Store, and the Homewood Motor Company, a dealer in Ford and Lincoln products managed by William Bennett. On the second floor, Dr. George Scupham and dentist Carl Harmke established their offices.

Across the street on the southeast corner of the Dixie Highway and Main Street, realtor Frank Prindiville opened his office in the old Buggert home in 1924. By 1929, the house was demolished to make room for the construction of the "Dixie-Ridge" Building, its identity reflecting the change of Main Street's name to Ridge Road in 1928. The Dixie-Ridge Building was completed in October 1929, and a gala open house was held on the twelfth of that month. Numbered as tenants in the new building were George Alexander's Sweet Shop—a candy store, luncheonette, and soda fountain in the corner space; Fred Tatgenhorst's Dixie-Ridge Barber Shop; George May's first jewelry store in town; the Monarch Laundry; the Tobias Novelty Shop—specializing in women's and men's notions; and the Homewood Recreation Parlor—a bowling alley, billiard and pool hall owned by Fred and George Hartmann. The second floor of the building included a number of "deluxe" apartments.

Delivery wagon in front of the Guaranteed Fuel and Supply Company. The company's yard was located on the site where Millennium Park now sits on Harwood Avenue. *(Marge Baker)*

By the end of the decade, Homewood's main intersection, the Dixie Highway and

The "Homewood" Building, a landmark to this day at Ridge Road and Dixie Highway, was completed in 1925. Homewood's first traffic light is also pictured.

Ridge Road, was touted as having the "most modern business buildings in Cook County south of Chicago." The same three buildings still anchor the intersection today.

Construction of other modern buildings occurred throughout Homewood's expanding business district. The Illinois Bell Telephone Company built a larger building to house its switchboard on Ridge Road just east of Gottschalk Avenue in 1927. More operators were needed to connect the increasing number of calls placed by Homewood residents. Farther west on Ridge Road, in 1922, William Warning built a two-story building (2012) to house his hardware store. Warning, who had taken over Theodore Witt's general store on the northeast corner of Main and Martin in 1909, sold this business to concentrate on selling hardware. Warning sold the general store to William Clothier who operated it until 1942. In 1924, south on the Dixie Highway, Bert Heuer erected an auto repair garage and service station where he also dealt in the sale of new Chevrolets.

The "Dixie-Ridge" Building, another present-day landmark, was completed in 1929, a year after Main Street was renamed Ridge Road.

A year later, in 1925, the Neutrowound Radio Manufacturing Company, a division of the Advanced Automobile Accessories Corporation, moved their production facilities from Chicago to Homewood. Their plant was located in a new 50' x 300' building south of the Homewood Coal, Ice and Material Company yard located on 183rd Street west of the I.C. tracks. In addition to producing radio sets in fine wood cabinetry, Neutrowound also produced a uniquely styled ultra modern set in a metal case that required three dials to fine tune.

To help boost sales, Neutrowound purchased its own radio station, WCBZ, which had been operated by the Cappotelli Brothers Music House in Chicago Heights. Neutrowound moved the station to broadcast and transmission facilities adjacent to its plant in Homewood, and the Federal Radio Commission (FRC) allowed the station to operate at 500 watts and assigned the station call letters WOK.

WOK frequently broadcast live remote programs from studios in the Terrace Garden Room of the Morrison Hotel at Clark and Madison Streets in Chicago. These remote broadcasts were prone to technical difficulties, which required a great deal of coordination between station staff at the studio and the transmission facilities in Homewood to correct. It was dur-

Bert Heuer completed construction of his new Homewood Service Garage building on Dixie Highway south of Ridge Road in 1924. *(Bert Heuer)*

ing one of these remotes on July 11, 1926, that vibrations from applause after the completion of a dance number caused a fuse to blow back at the station's transmitter in Homewood. On duty at the transmitter, nineteen-year-old Lester Wolf, said to be one of the youngest licensed radio operators in the country, sprang into action, and began to replace the blown fuse when he was knocked down by a jolt of electricity. When chief operator Herbert Pomy reached Wolf, the young man had regained his footing but collapsed and died minutes later. In his haste to effect repairs, Wolf had failed to disconnect the power.

Advertisement for the Neutrowound Radio Manufacturing Company *(Debbie Michalowski)*

Lester Wolf was the first person to die in broadcasting, and radio station WRNY in New York City began raising funds to erect a monument in his honor. Although some money was raised, it was later believed to have been stolen, and the monument never became a reality. Wolf is buried in Homewood Memorial Gardens, and a modest stone marks his grave with a simple inscription that reads: "A Martyr to Radio."

Neutrowound Radio Manufacturing ceased operation in Homewood in 1928, and the firm was sold to the Potter Company in 1929. Trianon, Inc. purchased WOK in 1927. Trianon, owner of the famous ballroom by the same name at 6201 S. Cottage Grove Avenue in Chicago, also owned station WMBB (World's Most Beautiful Ballroom). WOK and WMBB operated jointly for about a year until the stations were denied renewal of their licenses in 1928. After a number of appeals, the Federal Radio Commission's action was upheld by a federal court decision in 1931, which signaled the end of operation for Homewood's only commercial radio broadcast station.

A couple of blocks north of the Neutrowound plant on Harwood Avenue, two Tudor-style buildings were built in 1928 that still are landmarks on the street to this day. One building, currently home to Aurelio's Pizza, was built for Jack Kurtz to house his Superior Service Garage, an auto repair facility, which also served as a dealership for the Pontiac Motor Company. Across the street, the Hibbing brothers built the building at 18123 Harwood that served as home for their feed store. The name of Morris Avenue north of Olive Road was changed to Harwood Avenue in 1928 to honor the late Roderick Bannister Harwood who had served on the village board and in the volunteer fire department and who had owned a house on the street.

The decade was also marked by the construction of new schools and a number of major municipal improvements. By the end of the teens, the Standard School was "bulging at the seams." Cloakrooms were converted to classrooms, and the old Zimmer home on the southwest corner of Martin and Main Streets was rented to house the primary grades. Students shared the house with Foskett's Undertaking Chapel, later Cordt's Funeral Home, and school days were sometimes abbreviated to allow time for wakes and funeral services.

To alleviate overcrowding, the school board purchased four acres at Highland Avenue and Main Street, and bonds were issued to finance the construction of a second school building. This school, named Central School, was completed in May 1923 and consisted of three classrooms, an office, and an auditorium. By 1928, eight classrooms, a gymnasium, and locker rooms were added to the building to accommodate the ever-growing numbers of school-age children in town.

Central School on Highland Avenue south of Ridge Road as it appeared after construction was completed in 1923.

Salem Lutheran School (left) was built in 1927, two years after the church was completed. The school building still stands at 18332 Morris Avenue.

In addition to the Central School, two parochial schools were also constructed during the decade. The Salem Lutheran Church established a day school in their original church building after the congregation's second church was completed in 1925. The school opened on September 8 of that year with twenty-one students enrolled under the instruction of Pastor Louis Schwartzkopf. By 1927, forty-seven pupils were crowded into the old church/school building, and plans were started for construction of a brick schoolhouse on Morris Avenue. The new Salem Lutheran School was dedicated on December 11, 1927.

St. Joseph's also established a school for the children of their congregation in 1926. Under the auspices of Father Stephen Sullivan, a

After St. Joseph Catholic School (left) was completed in 1926, the front portion of the church was veneered with matching brick, and a brick steeple was also added to the church.

two-and-one-half-story brick school was constructed north of the church on the Dixie Highway. Construction was started in May and completed by the fall of 1926. Seventy-two pupils were enrolled in the school, and these students were taught by three Dominican Sisters from Adrian, Michigan, under the leadership of Sr. Mary James Marsh, the school's principal. For many years, the sisters lived in quarters on the top floor of the school building.

In August 1926, the village board also embarked on an ambitious construction project. Plans were approved for the construction of sanitary and storm water sewers throughout the community along with the construction of a sewage disposal and purification plant to be built in the far southeast corner of the village. Although the project was completed in October 1927, the village had considerable concerns about the workmanship and withheld payment. The contractor sued the village, but through efforts largely attributed to Village Trustee Carl Menzel, an engineer by trade, the village mounted a successful defense and proved the defects alleged in the newly installed sewer piping. Legal wrangling concluded in 1929 when a judge rendered a verdict against the contractor, the Blackhawk Construction Company, and the system was finally repaired to the village's satisfaction.

During the remaining years of the decade, the village also completed a comprehensive street-paving program in which almost all streets in town that had not been previously paved were paved with concrete. New cement sidewalks were also installed in front of the many homes being built throughout the community.

The completion of these improvements was helpful in securing favorable action when Postmaster Frank Cowing submitted petitions to the postmaster general in Washington calling for home delivery of mail to all village residents. Washington approved the request on the condition that the village change to a street address plan consistent with the city of Chicago and its adjacent suburbs. Under this plan, all houses and buildings on north-south streets would be numbered from 17500 to 18900 while numbers on east-west streets would run from 800 starting at Halsted Street to 3200 ending at Kedzie Avenue. The village complied, and home mail delivery throughout town started on May 1, 1928. Remarkably, mail was delivered twice each day—once in the morning and then again in the afternoon—six days a week.

By the start of 1929, Homewood and the rest of the nation had experienced a decade of unprecedented prosperity. The *South Cook Courier*, in its New Year's edition, heralded 1929 as a year that would be "Rich in Promise." Little could anyone imagine that by year's end, the stock market would crash on "Black Tuesday" wiping out market gains and fortunes a decade in the making.

Ridge Road looking west from Dixie Highway, during the construction of storm and sanitary sewers along the street.

Dreary scene on Ridge Road looking east from Harwood Avenue ***(William F. Moore)***

CHAPTER 10
The Depression

The crash of the stock market on "Black Tuesday," October 29, 1929, initiated a precipitous decline in the nation's economy that plunged the country into a depression, which lasted much of the next decade. It was initially hoped the effects of the "crash" would be short-lived, and the markets would rebound. These hopes were dashed as conditions worsened and the economy continued to race downhill.

Unemployment, which affected 3 percent of the nation's workforce in 1929, soared to 25 percent in 1933, leaving more than fifteen million Americans out of work. With such high numbers jobless, people stopped spending money. Demand for durable goods like housing, cars, and appliances declined, and production faltered. By the end of 1932, output at American manufacturing plants had been cut in half from 1929 levels, and thousands of mills, factories, and other businesses were forced to close.

The banking system also teetered on collapse. Many banks had made loans to businesses and people who could no longer afford to repay them. Other banks had lost money by investing in the stock market. Depositors withdrew funds from their accounts at alarming rates, and some banks did not have the cash to meet these demands. By March 1933, thousands of banks had failed, wiping out the savings of millions of people.

The effects of the Great Depression were devastating. Many people who had lost their jobs remained out of work for years. Those who worked faced major pay cuts, and many could only find part-time jobs. Home foreclosures increased, which led to higher numbers of homeless. Families struggled to make ends meet, and children often took whatever work they could get to help support their households. Despair even caused some to turn to crime, which increased after the onset of the Depression.

View of Dixie Highway looking north at the Ridge Road intersection

Conditions weren't much better in Homewood. Many of the factories in Harvey, Chicago Heights, and the south side of Chicago that employed local residents laid off workers, cut production to a few days a week, or closed altogether. Homewood property owners faced a triple hardship. Not only were they worried about paying their mortgages and regular tax bills, but they also had to come up with their share of the over $600,000 in special assessments the village levied to help finance the sewer, street, and sidewalk improvements completed during the late 1920s.

Most homeowners tried desperately to meet the four special assessments when they became due, but when they failed to meet the first payment, the second payment with its accrued interest became so much larger. Then the third payment became larger still until many property owners found themselves with a debt they were unable to satisfy. The numbers of tax delinquent sales and mortgage foreclosures rose, and some residents lost their homes altogether while many more were threatened with the loss of their homes.

Decreased tax receipts caused the village government to search for cost-saving measures. Salaries of village police officers and other workers were cut, equipment purchases were postponed, and infrastructure improvements were cancelled until more funds became available. The school board also struggled with its finances. Like the village board, the school board was faced with uncollectible taxes, creditors appearing at their board meetings demanding money due them, and an inability to borrow more funds from local banks. Teachers' salaries were lowered, and kindergarten classes and athletic, music, and manual training programs were eliminated. To raise money needed to keep the schools open, the school board sold tax anticipation warrants to citizens able to afford them. The tax anticipation warrants provided the school board with funds to bridge the gap and to stay afloat during the periods between the semi-annual tax collections. As an additional aid, the Parent Teachers Association held "tag days" to raise funds to help buy textbooks, reference materials, and other needed equipment.

Banks and businesses also felt the pinch. After twenty-four years in operation, the Homewood State Bank became a casualty to the effects of the Depression. State auditors closed the bank on July 18, 1932, and the bank's directors, led by Henry Gottschalk, hoped to reorganize and reopen the bank shortly thereafter. Unfortunately, the debt burden from the construction of the bank's new building, completed in 1925, compounded their problems, and the bank never did reopen. Liquidation proceedings lasted about ten years, and in the end, account holders were repaid less than 50 percent of their deposits.

To help curb the banking crisis, President Franklin Roosevelt declared a "bank holiday" the day after he took office in March 1933 that forced all banks throughout the country to close temporarily. Roosevelt then pushed a number of reforms to strengthen the banking system and help restore the public's confidence in it. These reforms were passed by Congress in the Emergency Banking Bill of 1933 on March 9. Chief among the reforms passed was the establishment of the Federal Deposit Insurance Corporation (FDIC), organized to insure bank deposits up to $2,500. Banks that were members of the Federal Reserve System were required to join the FDIC and had to meet stringent underwriting requirements before they could reopen. The Cook County Trust and Savings Bank on Ridge Road closed, like all banks, on March 5. After making application to the FDIC, the bank was granted membership and was allowed by federal regulators to reopen on March 22. The Cook County Trust and Savings Bank remained solvent throughout the Depression and was wooed to the city of Harvey in 1937. Harvey's two banks had closed in 1932, and the city remained bankless for five years. Shareholders of the Cook County Trust and Savings Bank approved the purchase of the shuttered Bank of Harvey building at 174 E. 154th Street, and the bank moved its facilities to this location and opened for business under the new name, the First National Bank of Harvey, on March 8, 1937. The bank's former facilities in Homewood were then

The Cook County Trust and Savings Bank at Ridge Road and Dixie Highway remained solvent during the Depression.

After the Cook County Trust and Savings Bank moved to Harvey, the National Tea Food Store moved into the bank's space. ***(Cowing Collection)***

taken over by the National Tea Food Store. After the departure of the Cook County Trust and Savings Bank, Homewood remained without a bank until 1946.

Homewood's remaining financial institution, the Homewood Building and Loan, also weathered the storm of the Depression years and continued to operate without interruption. After the financial collapse of the Homewood State Bank, the Building and Loan was forced to move into offices at 2048 Ridge Road and remained at this location through the rest of the decade. The Federal Savings and Loan Insurance Corporation certified the Building and Loan, managed by Adolph Sommerfield, in October 1938, and all accounts were insured by the federal agency thereafter.

The Homewood State Bank wasn't the only business in town to succumb to the Depression. With little discretionary income to spend, fans stopped attending the dog races at the Illinois Kennel Club's facilities on Halsted Street. The track closed in 1934, never to reopen. With higher stakes and a more affluent clientele, the Washington Park Race Track fared much better, and horse racing continued.

Postcard advertisement for Feuer's Homewood Inn

The Amalfi Gardens, after a few years of adjusting its menu and prices to try to lure more diners, served its last meal in May 1935. A month later, the restaurant reopened as Ben's Chateau. Fine dining restaurants were hard-pressed to stay in business during the Depression, and Ben's closed after about a year. The restaurant was known as Feuer's Homewood Inn in 1937 and as the Reno Chateau owned by Joe Zarantonello in 1940.

On Ridge Road, the People's Dry Goods Store owned by Jacob Schwab's widow Fannie and Sachs' Drug Store both were foreclosed on in 1933 and 1935, respectively. Grocer Albert Hecht chose to close his store on Ridge Road in 1935 and retire rather than deal with the frustrations of running a business during this period. New owners subsequently reopened all of these stores.

On the Dixie Highway, Bert Heuer was forced to close his auto service garage in 1936. Like the Homewood State Bank, Heuer had to shoulder the added burden of paying off the note on his large garage building completed in 1924. Established auto repair businesses suffered greatly in the Depression, primarily due to an explosion in the numbers of unemployed "alley" mechanics who were doing auto repairs more cheaply with less overhead. The Schmidt brothers, who owned the Dixie Service Garage at 183rd Street and the Dixie Highway, were also forced to close their business. Irvin Ruge later reopened this garage, which he managed for over twenty years as Ruge's Super Service.

Elsewhere, the old Steiner mill on Harwood Avenue had been vacant since the Klin Brothers golf club factory closed in 1926. Economic conditions made it difficult to sell or rent the building, and the structure fell into disrepair. The mill became an "attractive nuisance" for neighborhood children and was also deemed a fire hazard. Reacting to numerous complaints, the state fire marshal ordered the building's demolition. After close to eighty years as a local landmark, the mill was torn down to the foundation walls in September 1934.

Heuer's Service Garage on Dixie Highway, south of Ridge Road, was a victim of the Depression like many other businesses in Homewood. ***(Bert Heuer)***

Top: **The Dixie Service Garage was located at 18301 Dixie Highway. The building has been enlarged over the years and is now home to Chuck's House of Magic.**

Following his inauguration, President Franklin Roosevelt also took strong steps to stem the rising tide of business failures, unemployment, and homelessness. After emergency-banking legislation was passed, Roosevelt turned his attention to seeing that Congress immediately enacted other measures that would stimulate almost every sector of the economy. Early legislation included the National Industrial Recovery Act, which established the National Recovery Administration (NRA), an agency that developed codes of fair competition to regulate business and to eliminate unfair pricing. Businesses who pledged themselves to these codes, developed with the help of various trade associations, could display the NRA blue eagle symbol in their store windows and on the packaging for their products. Almost all businesses in Homewood participated in this voluntary program, which was later declared unconstitutional in 1935.

To help put the unemployed back to work, the Civil Works Administration (CWA) was established in 1933. Large numbers of men were engaged in CWA-financed projects administered by local jurisdictions. In Homewood, the CWA provided funding for painting the exterior and interior of the village hall and library and for painting all fire hydrants in town. The village also used CWA manpower for street and sewer improvement and maintenance projects and for snow plowing. The school board utilized CWA funding and workmen for painting projects at both Standard and Central Schools and to re-roof and upgrade the heating and electrical systems at Standard School.

The Civil Works Administration was abolished in 1935 when the Works Progress Administration (WPA) was set up to complete similar public improvement projects. The WPA also sponsored public art, music, and writing projects in communities throughout the country. In Homewood, WPA funds were used to finance athletic, dance, music, drama, acrobatic, and other recreational programs for adults and children. These activities were held at various locations including St. Paul Church, Gottschalk's Pavilion, and Central and Standard Schools. Many people fondly remember the acrobatic and gymnastic lessons they received from Joe Sells as part of the federal recreation program. Sells was well qualified to instruct these classes. He had spent thirty-five years as a performer in his family's business, the Sells-Floto Circus.

Village President Fred Borgwardt, standing with axe in hand, and other village officials pose in front of Homewood's original village hall just before the building was torn down in 1938 to clear land for the construction of a new municipal building.

The relief agency that was to have the most lasting impact on the village of Homewood was the Public Works Administration (PWA). PWA funds were used to construct major projects including dams, roads, and buildings. In 1935, PWA funds were used to construct a water softening plant and a 250,000-gallon storage tank at the village's waterworks next to the village hall. The water tower, the second half of the project, was completed by the Chicago Bridge and Iron Company in May 1935 and still stands behind the village hall. The water softening plant became obsolete when Chicago water replaced well water in village taps in 1983. The building the plant was housed in was torn down in 1998 to make room for an addition to the village hall.

PWA funds were also used to build a new village hall and auditorium beginning in 1938. For years, village officials had felt the old village hall was inadequate. The question of building a new hall was put to voters in 1930, but the proposal was soundly rejected. Village fathers were wary about putting the question to a vote again, especially in the midst of the Depression, but the federal government made $5 billion in PWA funding available for projects like this in the summer of 1938. Village trustees felt this was an offer too good to refuse. The village board acted quickly, and in a special meeting held on July 26, they passed an ordinance calling for a referendum on a bond issue for the proposed municipal building. The referendum date was set for September 8.

Village President Fred Borgwardt, lower left facing camera, watches as the cornerstone is placed for Homewood's new village hall in 1939.

Even with government funding of $61,363, taxpayers were asked to approve bond sales in the amount of $74,000 to help finance construction of a new building. Many residents could not see the logic of assuming the tax burden on a building far bigger than their small town would ever need. Others argued the village had just spent money to upgrade the electrical wiring and replace the boiler in the old village hall just two years before, and the old hall was good enough for the town. The debate continued, but after votes were tallied on September 8, the "yes" side won by just seventeen votes—490 to 473.

With the question decided, the village board sprang into action as timing was of critical importance. One of the provisions of the PWA grant was the completion of the building within one year after the referendum and that actual construction work should start within twelve weeks. Unfortunately, the old village hall occupied the site of the new building. The old hall had to be demolished, and village offices had to be moved. In a textbook example of intergovernmental cooperation, board meetings were held at Central School, prisoners were taken to the Flossmoor jail, and the village clerk's office was moved into space in the water softening building. The village fire truck was housed around the corner on Dixie Highway in Severson's Garage for a fee of $15 per month.

Foundation work on the new building started in December 1938, and by August 1939, the village board was holding meetings in the

Homewood's current village hall after construction was completed in 1939.

council chambers on the second floor of the completed building. Spacious quarters for the fire department, police department, and village clerk's staff were now available all under one roof. The building also included a three-hundred-seat auditorium with a hardwood basketball court, stage, and kitchen to be used for community entertainment and recreational purposes.

A formal dedication was held on Saturday, September 30, 1939. The ceremonies, entitled "An Evening of Friendliness," included a concert held by the community band directed by J. Norman Beasley, a program of speakers led by Village President Fred Borgwardt, and dancing with music provided by Norman Woody and his Music Masters. Refreshments consisting of two barrels of beer donated by Fred Gold and $28.80 worth of ice cream rounded out the night's festivities. With remodeling completed in 1968 and 1998, Homewood's village hall and auditorium still serve the community well after sixty-five years.

The last major PWA project completed in Homewood was the post office building at 1921 Ridge Road. Built during the spring and summer of 1940 at a cost of $75,000, the modern brick facility replaced the old Mueller farmhouse, which had stood on the site since the mid-1800s.

Homewood's Community Band played at many village functions, including the dedication of the village hall in 1939. J. Norman Beasley directed the band for many years.

The post office, headed by Postmaster William Cato, was dedicated on October 26, 1940. Prior to the construction of this structure, the post office had been located at 18109 Dixie Highway since May 1936.

In addition to putting local men to work, these relief efforts also helped moderate the increase in criminal activity, which had grown alarmingly during the first years of the Depression. Within months of the crash, Homewood was the scene of a brazen daylight robbery at the village's post office, then located at 2005 Ridge Road. On a quiet Saturday in April 1930, postal clerk Joseph Tobias had just finished a transaction with Mrs. Fred Adam when he noticed a man loitering around the writing desk in the front lobby. After Mrs. Adam left the building, the man brandished a pistol and announced a holdup. Tobias complied with his requests, and as he did this, an accomplice entered the front door to the post office. Tobias was bound and gagged, and a mailbag was placed over his head. The post office safe, which was open for the day's business, was then looted of $6,436.29 in stamps and $105.95 in cash.

Excavation work is underway for the Homewood Post Office, 1921 Ridge Road.

As the bandits exited the rear door, Joe Sells, another postal employee, had just driven into the courtyard behind the building. Sells noticed the men wearing hats and long overcoats and that one was carrying a sawed-off shotgun while the other was carrying the mail sack. Sells, initially surprised by this, assumed the men were new guards assigned to transport registered mail pouches. He quickly realized his error when the men began to sprint to their "high powered Chrysler" getaway car. Sells dashed into the post office and found Tobias bound and gagged. He then ran out onto Ridge Road to sound the alarm. Homewood Patrolman Harry Sundeen was nearby and raced to the area on foot. Sundeen noticed the getaway car beginning to head west on Cherry Lane for Martin Avenue. He also noticed Henry Gottschalk beginning to back his car out of his garage onto Cherry Lane. Sundeen hopped onto the running board of Gottschalk's car and ordered a

The Homewood Post Office after construction was completed in October 1940.

pursuit. Gottschalk, startled and unaware as to what was happening, stalled the car and could not restart it. Sundeen quickly commandeered another car and took up the pursuit of the bandits who had traveled south on Martin Avenue and then west onto 183rd Street. Sundeen was soon joined in the chase by the Homewood police car driven by Officer Herb Kitterer and by the Cook County Highway Police. Some Homewood citizens also joined in on the chase west to Cicero Avenue and then north towards Chicago. Martin Avenue resident Henry Rathje and his son Theodore, who had witnessed the robbery and getaway unfold near their home, also took up the pursuit. The Rathjes, however, ended up going south on the Governors Highway before deciding to give up their efforts near Monee.

Sundeen, Kitterer, and their band chased the suspects on Cicero Avenue to the Rock Island tracks where they learned from a railroad watchman that a car matching the description of the suspect vehicle had passed the tracks just moments before. Although still hot on the bandits' trail, a passenger train's approach blocked the crossing and squelched any further attempt to pursue the getaway car. The patrolmen returned to Homewood empty-handed.

Homewood police officer directs traffic at Ridge and Dixie in front of the Community Pharmacy and Homewood Building.

Scenes similar to this were being repeated in hundreds of small towns across the country. Newspapers chronicled the exploits of notorious bank robbers like Bonnie and Clyde, John Dillinger, "Pretty Boy" Floyd, and others. Near Homewood, in 1930 alone, banks had been robbed in Frankfort, Beecher, Crete, Matteson, and Monee. Homewood village officials and business owners vowed the town's two banks would not fall victim to robbers as the post office had. With village approval, the businesses established a "town guard" to augment the police force; five downtown business owners were given shotguns, and their buildings were wired to alarm buttons in the banks.

This view of the intersection of Dixie Highway and Ridge Road was taken in the late 1930s.

Once activated, the alarms set off bells in the designated businesses signaling their owners to a problem at one of the banks. The town guards, with shotguns in hand, were then supposed to respond to check on the trouble. Bert Heuer, Al Gold, and Henry Bernard were three of the town guards appointed. Fortunately, the town guards never had to fire a shot. Homewood may not have been an attractive target for a bank robbery—not so much for the deterrence posed by the town guards but by the fact the Cook County Trust and Savings Bank had extensively fortified its facilities with bulletproof glass and steel plating, and the Homewood State Bank had closed its doors, going into receivership in 1932, thereby reducing the potential targets in town to one.

Officer Al Toberman stands beside the village's 1930 Ford Model "A" squad car. ***(Susan White)***

Homewood's police force led by Chief Walter Gleason, a department veteran since 1904, consisted of three patrolmen for much of the decade—William Utermark, Albert Toberman, and Fred Nyquist. These officers were kept quite busy during the Depression years. Constantly on watch to prevent another robbery at the post office or one of the banks, the officers also had to deal with a tremendous influx of unemployed wandering through town. These tramps and hobos frequently "rode the rails" of the Illinois Central, and as freight trains stopped at the Markham Yards, they wandered into Homewood. In a preemptive measure, Homewood patrolmen would detain these vagrants as night fell to prevent them from causing any troubles in town. The vagrants were given a place to sleep for the night in the village calaboose and a "cup of coffee and two rolls" in the morning before being ushered out of town.

A logbook kept by the department of the "night lodgers" housed in the jail makes it clear these men were not prisoners, and the logbook shows the dramatic increase in the numbers housed during the early years of the Depression. In 1930, the number of men lodged for the year amounted to 630; this number increased to 1,669 in 1931, subsequently decreased to 1,224 in 1933, and then to 298 in 1939. Conditions and treatment must not have been too bad in Homewood.

The logbook recorded the lodger's name, address (if any), age,

Officer William Utermark, Chief Walter Gleason, and Officer Al Toberman stand in front of the police department's new 1935 Plymouth patrol car. *(Susan White)*

next of kin, and occupation (if any). While it would not have been unusual to have hobos or tramps coming from locales along the Illinois Central main line, many found their way to Homewood from places like Los Angeles, San Francisco, Vancouver, Tampa, New York, and Boston, in addition to hundreds of smaller towns all across the country.

Homewood police and federal agents were also kept busy dealing with illegal "stills" in town. While Prohibition was repealed in 1933, thirteen years after it took effect, poor economic conditions continued to make bootlegging profitable. In May 1937, Homewood police assisted federal alcohol agents in the raid of a home at 189th Street and Dixie Highway. There they found a 350-gallon still and 10,000 gallons of mash. The owner was taken into custody, and it was determined that he had been arrested several months before in Glenwood on the same charges. Months later on October 2, another raid was conducted on a home in the 1600 block of Linden Road. There, officers and "feds" found a 250-gallon still and 3,600 gallons of mash. Underground pipes connected the still in the home with a garage on the property and with another garage on a neighboring lot on Ridge Road. Homewood police conducted their final raid on an "alky" operation in July 1938. Police Chief Gleason and his men initiated this raid in the 1300 block of Olive Road and seized a 300-gallon still and a 3,000-gallon vat of mash cleverly concealed in a subcellar. Federal alcohol tax agents were notified and came to the scene the following morning to wreck the still and destroy the mash.

Despite activity like this, crime, overall, was not that bad in Homewood. In addition to the regular police force and the town guards, the Cook County Sheriff's Police also had had a substation in Homewood since the mid-1920s, which bolstered police presence in town. The station was initially located in a converted railcar near the intersection of Dixie Highway and the

The Cook County Sheriff's Police station was completed in 1937 at 1154 Ridge Road. ***(Cowing Collection)***

Egyptian Trail (Park Avenue). New facilities, complete with the area's first two-way police radio station and transmitter, were completed in 1937 at 1154 Ridge Road. The sheriff's police operated out of this facility until it was closed in 1975.

All the news during the Depression was not full of doom and gloom. The Homewood Businessmen's Association and other organizations, like the volunteer fire department and the American Legion, sponsored festivities to help take people's minds off the stresses of the Depression. "Plae Daes" were held each year at one of the local golf clubs to allow villagers to enjoy a day of golf, swimming, and tennis. Many families also participated in annual picnic excursions to Cedar Lake, Indiana. A full day of activities was planned for these events, which started with a caravan of autos carrying participants from Homewood to Cedar Lake. In 1933, Homewoodians, like many others throughout the country, also looked forward to trips to the Chicago World's Fair known as a "Century of Progress" Exhibition. A trip to the fair, which ran from May 27 through November 1, was a perfect way for folks to escape from the troubles and burdens they faced each day during the Depression. The fair was meant to celebrate Chicago's centennial and was also an exhibition to showcase improvements and advancements in science and technology.

Anticipating record attendance, many Chicago suburbs, like Homewood, used the fair as an opportunity to promote commerce and interest in their own communities. Homewood established a World's Fair Committee to coordinate the village's promotional efforts. Elmer McKee, who was assisted by other members including Alvin Gold, Shirley Cowing, W. Mac Miller, and Ernest Waibel, chaired the committee. The committee arranged for the construction of an information cabin on a lot on the northwest corner of Dixie Highway and Ridge Road, which was vacant at the time. Volunteers staffed the cabin and provided tourists traveling through town with fair, food, lodging, and

Homewood's 1933 World's Fair promotional brochure

transportation information. A major goal of the committee was to encourage tourists to use Homewood as a base for their visits to the fair. Village residents were encouraged to rent out their spare rooms to guests during the months the fair was open, and the information cabin served as a clearinghouse for available rooms. A promotional flyer was also produced and distributed to points south and east of town extolling the virtues of staying in Homewood, chief of which was Homewood's access to Illinois Central trains, which would whisk passengers to the Exhibition in thirty minutes.

Although the Dixie Highway was a direct route to the fairgrounds, the hordes of visitors the village anticipated never materialized. The fair's publicity department, fearing unmanageable congestion on many of the direct routes, published directions diverting traffic around Homewood using alternate routes like Illinois Route 50 (Cicero Avenue), U.S. Route 45 (LaGrange Road), U.S. Route 6 (159th Street), and Illinois Route 1 (Halsted Street). In the end, the economic impact of the fair was not that great in Homewood.

After only four months in operation, the information cabin in Homewood was sold and moved off the property in early September 1933. Edward Dugdale then developed the lot as a gas station and opened his Shell "Lubritorium" later that year. After a few years, Jack Kurtz took over the station and sold Sinclair brand gasoline there for the next five decades.

Jack Kurtz stands in front of his service station on the northwest corner of Ridge Road and Dixie Highway. ***(Charlotte Kurtz)***

Later in the Depression, the businessmen, firefighters, and legionnaires also sponsored the annual "Homewood Homecoming"—several days of events leading up to the Fourth of July, which included a carnival, street dances, and a large parade held on the Fourth. The "Homecomings" were always popular and continued for years after the Depression ended.

Through hard work and perseverance, most home and business owners were able to hold on to their properties, and many new businesses even opened and prospered during the Depression years. In 1930, Morse Van Drunen and partner John Rearick took over operation of the Homewood Motor Company at 18029 Dixie Highway and established the Van Drunen-Rearick Ford Agency. Van Drunen later became sole owner of the business, which is currently owned by his grandson Marvin Van Drunen. Van Drunen moved his dealership to the corner of 183rd Street and Dixie Highway in 1951, and the company moved to its current location on 183rd Street west of Kedzie Avenue in 1973.

Van Drunen Ford's first showroom, opened in 1930, was located at 18029 Dixie Highway. ***(Van Drunen Ford)***

With repeal of Prohibition in 1933, beer flowed again legally in Homewood. Louis Mueller Jr. reopened his father's tavern at 2060 Ridge Road while across the street at 2059 Ridge Road, Ernie Sanders added "real" beer and hard liquor to his restaurant's menu. Farther east on Ridge, Oliver Homer opened Homer's Home Tavern in the former Warning Hardware Store at 2012 Ridge Road. A month after repeal took effect, businessman Fred Gold and his sons also became the exclusive distributors for Budweiser beer and the Anheuser-Busch Brewing Company in south Cook County. Warehouse facilities were located on the site of the Homewood Coal, Ice and Material yard they owned on 183rd Street. Their distributorship, known then as the Homewood Beverage Company, was the predecessor to the Chicago Beer Distributing Company, currently located on 167th Street in Markham.

Morse Van Drunen stands inside his showroom displaying Ford's 1931 models. ***(Van Drunen Ford)***

By 1935, the effects of the Depression moderated, and other businesses opened. The Pyramid Foods Company purchased the long-vacant Neutrowound Radio Manufacturing plant where they began making malted candy. By the end of the decade, the plant would be sold again to the Parsons Ammonia Company, who would produce household ammonia there until the early 1960s. The vacant building would later burn down in a spectacular fire in July 1967.

In March 1935, Ed Gittersonke opened the Royal Blue Grocery Store in the space Albert Hecht vacated at 2057 Ridge Road while in July, Robert Lewis opened his hardware store at 18033 Dixie Highway.

Lewis built a new building for his store in the early 1950s at 1940 Ridge Road and remained in business here until he retired in the mid-1970s.

Two businesses that opened in November 1937 testified to the hope of many that the Depression would soon end. The Homewood Credit Union was organized that month under the leadership of President Edgar Laybourne, Vice President Joseph Swingle, and Treasurer Richard Gansbergen. Within months, membership and deposits had grown, which gave credence to the fact that residents had regained their faith in thrift institutions and now had discretionary income to invest.

On November 23, villagers turned out in large numbers for the grand opening of the Homewood Theatre. The crowds were treated to the musical comedy *Double or Nothing* starring Bing Crosby and Martha Raye. Regular admission was twenty-five cents. The 659-seat theatre was constructed by remodeling the shuttered Heuer's Service Garage building on Dixie Highway south of Ridge Road. The $75,000 "motion picture palace" had all the latest amenities for the comfort of its patrons and was one of the first buildings in town to be air-conditioned. The theatre was operated by the firm of Jones, Linick and Schafer, veteran Chicago movie exhibitors, who also ran the State-Lake, Dearborn, LaSalle, Woods, and McVicker's theatres downtown. Ken Dickinson was given the job of managing the Homewood movie house, a job he held for many years.

Ridge Road looking east from Martin Avenue in the late 1930s *(Chicago Sun-Times)*

The Homewood Theatre weathered good times and bad until it was closed in the early 1980s—a victim, like so many theatres in downtowns all across the country, to the competition of multiscreen cineplexes in new shopping malls. Plans to convert the theatre into a performing arts center never came to fruition, and the building was torn down in the spring of 1992 to make way for a municipal parking lot.

As the decade neared an end, the country began to recover. Around Homewood, factories in Chicago Heights and Harvey increased production and hired more workers. The outlook seemed brighter, but the "winds of war" were blowing in Europe, casting storm clouds across the Atlantic.

Above: View looking north on Dixie to Ridge Road in December 1937

Middle: The Homewood Theatre shortly after it opened in November 1937

Below: Another view of the Homewood Theatre and the west side of Dixie Highway south of Ridge Road in the late 1930s

Once the Homewood Hotel was demolished, this building at 2009 Ridge Road housing the National Tea Food Store was built in its place. *(William F. Moore)*

Top: Demolition work begins on the old Homewood Hotel on Ridge Road just west of Dixie Highway. *(William F. Moore)*

CHAPTER 11
The War Years

The first years of the forties were full of renewed optimism. Unemployment decreased as manufacturing increased. Income levels rose, which led to greater consumer spending. The nation began to lift itself out of the Depression, which buoyed the spirits of all Americans. In Homewood, home building resumed after many dormant years, a clear indication that prosperous times lay ahead.

Following the lead of Chicago meatpacking magnate Nelson Swift Morris, who built a sprawling fourteen-room Spanish Mission-style residence on the north end of Perth Avenue, other well-to-do families began building homes in Homewood also. During 1940 and 1941, fifty new houses were erected in town, but none was as elaborate as the Morris mansion. Morris, a World War I veteran who was an original signer of the American Legion charter in Paris and a survivor of the May 1937 *Hindenburg* disaster, was a member of the Ravisloe Country Club and owned acreage west of the golf course grounds. His home, completed in 1937, was a gift to his second wife Blanche Bilboa, a well-known French stage actress and heir to the Coty family, internationally renowned makers of fine perfumes and cosmetics. Nineteen forty also saw the completion of a new building in the 2000 block of Ridge Road, which housed a number of businesses including the Ben Franklin five-and-ten-cent store and Twietmeyer's Dairy Bar. By the end of the decade, the Homewood Hotel was demolished in this same block, and the National Tea store moved to a new and larger building that was built in the hotel's place.

After a decade of struggles and economic stagnation, Homewood's future looked bright. To celebrate, the Homewood Homecoming festivities of 1941 were larger than usual, and the whole town seemed to immerse

The American Legion's famous "Leaping Lena" delights crowds of onlookers on the Dixie Highway during the Homewood Homecoming celebration of 1941.

Top: **Cowboys and Indians parade on horseback up Dixie Highway in the 1941 Homewood Homecoming celebration.**

itself into the pioneer theme set for the celebration. Men grew mustaches and beards, and men and women alike dressed in period garb reminiscent of the mid-1850s when Homewood was a fledgling settlement. The Homecoming of 1941, however, was to be the last one marked by such gaiety for a number of years to come.

Dampening enthusiasm were reports that filled the radio and newspapers daily of the war that had broken out in Europe following Germany's invasion of Poland on September 1, 1939. After this, Britain and France declared war on Germany, setting the stage for another world conflict. Many Americans, weary from a decade of the Depression and wary of becoming involved in another great war, pushed for the United States to stay out of this conflict. News of the war grew direr for the Allied powers when Germany invaded France in June 1940 and Nazi planes began to bombard England. The United States reacted to this grim news by requiring all men between the ages of twenty-one and thirty-five years to register for the draft in October 1940. Over sixteen million American men were registered.

Through 1941, the conflict worsened. The German army invaded the Soviet Union while the Japanese invaded areas throughout Asia. Relations between the United States and Japan crumbled, and it became increasingly evident that Americans could not avoid becoming embroiled in the war. Any uncertainty about the necessity of the United States' involvement ended on Sunday, December 7, 1941, the infamous date when United States installations at Pearl Harbor, Hawaii, were "suddenly and deliberately attacked by naval and air forces of the Empire of Japan." The following day, Japan attacked the main American base in the Philippines, and the United States declared war. Three days later, war was declared on Germany and Italy, the remaining Axis powers.

Outraged, young men and women throughout the country flooded recruitment offices and volunteered for service with the armed forces. By June 1942, 112 names of young men serving in the war were inscribed on a Roll of Honor hung in the entranceway of the Homewood Village Hall. As the war ground on, this roll would grow to include the names of over 200 men and women. Brothers, sons, fathers, and daughters were all among the names listed. Many families in town had more than one member defending their country. Brothers Eugene, Charles, and Joseph Klauk; Sidney, William, and Alfred Steiner; William, Howard, and Albert Zilske; Irvin, Jack, and Roy Cofran; William, Karl, and Lewis Turlay; Cornelius, Clarence, and Robert Baker; Arthur, Thomas, and Robert Welsh; Tom and Henry Puhrmann; Henry and Fred Utermark; and Oscar and Herbert Nietfeldt were all among the young men from Homewood heeding the call to arms. Sisters Mary Frances and Betty Marie Prindiville; brothers and sisters Beryl, Marie, and Walter Laird; Edna and Edward Goesel; Margaret and Jack Jabrosky; and father and son Earl Multog Sr. and Earl Jr. were also among those from Homewood serving on many fronts.

Bon Voyage party for sailor Earl Multog Jr., top row center, was given before he left for service in the U.S. Navy. The date—December 6, 1941.

The Utermark boys, Henry, left, and Fred, right, stand beside their father, Homewood police officer William Utermark early in World War II. ***(Emma McLean)***

The Thomas family: Ray, Don, Florence, father Harry (rear); Charlotte, Steve (center); Paul, Farrell, Jack (front). Six of the Thomas boys including son Harry, not pictured, served their country in World War II. ***(Mariann Reilly)***

No family, however, could best the record of Harry and Florence Thomas, who sent six sons, Farrell, Raymond, Harry, Donald, Jack, and Paul into harm's way. Although Raymond would be wounded in Okinawa, and Farrell would be held in a German prisoner of war camp for ten months after being captured in France, all the Thomas boys returned home safely at war's end. Other families were not as fortunate.

During World War II, thirteen young men from Homewood made the supreme sacrifice. Adding to the grief over lost loved ones and friends, many in Homewood also mourned the deaths of seven other soldiers who had formerly lived in town and the three men from Flossmoor who never returned.

Walter Burns was the first from Homewood to give his life in the war. Burns had a keen desire to fly, and after the outbreak of the war in Europe, he attempted to enlist in the United States Army Air Corps.

Walter Burns (center) stands with other RCAF pilots while training in Canada. ***(Peggy Burns)***

Rejected because of his short stature, Walter enlisted with the Royal Canadian Air Force (RCAF) in October 1940. He achieved his dream to fly and was assigned to pilot a bomber in North Africa. While there, disaster struck on July 13, 1942, as Burns and his crew were returning from a mission. Four miles short of a desert landing strip, Burns' Wellington aircraft crashed after running out of fuel. He and the three other RCAF airmen on board the plane were killed. News of Walter's death reached Homewood a week later and shocked the community. "Wally" Burns was well known to many in town from his days working at the soda fountain in the Community Pharmacy. His death at the age of twenty-one drove the realities of war home, and many prayed his would be the last Homewood would endure.

Fate was not so kind. Although there would be no deaths of Homewood servicemen in the balance of 1942 and for all of 1943, the Allied offensives of 1944 and 1945 would certainly take their toll.

Parades helped to boost morale and patriotism during World War II. This parade heading west on Ridge Road at Dixie Highway was held on July 4, 1942.

In February 1944, reports of Homewood's second war death reached the village. Walter Richards of Ridge Road had been killed in action while serving aboard a minesweeper in the Mediterranean in January. Richards was twenty-nine years old and had been employed by the Homewood Post Office before enlisting in 1942. Several months later, on May 19, Lester B. Tienstra, age twenty, was killed when the B-24 Liberator bomber he was aboard crashed in Romania returning from a mission. Following the D-Day invasion, Edward Goesel, another twenty-year-old Homewood airman, was killed June 18 when his B-17 Flying Fortress was shot down over Germany. Farther south in Italy, Ivan Winslow was mortally wounded advancing with his infantry unit on the Anzio beachhead on June 14. Robert Downey was the final serviceman from Homewood killed in 1944. The twenty-one-year-old was killed in fierce combat attacking German pillboxes on the Seigfried line near Riesdorf, Germany.

As fighting continued into 1945, the Germans were in retreat, but the bloody battles of the Pacific continued. The battle for Iwo Jima in the western Pacific was to be the last fighting 6,821 Americans, including three young Marines from Homewood, would ever see. Privates Charles Henry, nineteen, Robert Johnson, twenty-two, and Walter Johnston, twenty-six, were all killed while battling for the island stronghold in February and March 1945. The death of Robert Johnson was particularly poignant. Johnson, an only child, died the same day, March 4, as Charles Henry, and he was a good friend and Cedar Road neighbor of Robert Downey, who was killed at the end of 1944. Corporal John Piani of the Third Armored Division of the First Army was Homewood's only combat death in the European Theater in 1945. He was killed fighting in Germany on March 30.

Karl Turlay was one of several young Homewood servicemen held captive in German prisoner of war camps. *(Lewis Turlay)*

In addition to those killed, many Homewood men were wounded in the war and were fortunate to return home alive. Like Farrell Thomas, five others were captured and held in German prisoner of war camps. Edward O'Brien, Karl Turlay, Raymond Hellstrom, Reuben Thode, and William Zilske all spent time as prisoners. O'Brien was captured after bailing out of his plane following a bombing raid over Bremen, Germany, in April 1943. Initially reporting good treatment by his captors, O'Brien indicated as the war progressed and Germany's gains were reversed that treatment in the camps worsened. Prior to his liberation in May 1945, O'Brien and others in his camp came close to starvation. Food items being sent by the Red Cross to the camp had been pilfered by German civilians and were being sold on the black market.

This treatment was in sharp contrast to the conditions in prisoner of war camps in the United States. One such camp was located south

Memorial Day Parade heads north on Dixie Highway near Chestnut Road, May 30, 1943.

of Thornton in the Sweet Woods Forest Preserve. A former Civilian Conservation Corps facility used during the Depression, the camp opened in January 1945 and, at its height, housed about 150 German prisoners. Due to a shortage of workers in the area during the war, the prisoners were transported daily to various farms and manufacturing plants where they were used as manual laborers. The prisoners were paid eighty cents a day in scrip that they could use in their camp's canteen. In Homewood, German prisoners worked on farms adjacent to town and also did chores at the Homewood Farms Dairy located on 175th Street near the Governors Highway.

During the time the camp was open, there was only one recorded escape. A twenty-year-old prisoner escaped in September 1945, and despite "federal, county and state police engaged in a widespread manhunt," he remained at large for eight days. To the surprise of employees at the Homewood Farms Dairy, the escapee appeared there on September 25 and surrendered to owner Fred Twietmeyer. The prisoner had previously worked at the dairy on a work release program and trusted Twietmeyer. As the war had already ended, he told Twietmeyer he feared he would be made a "slave laborer" when sent back to Germany, and he escaped only to be able to stay in the United States. The camp closed in February 1946, and remaining prisoners were sent to Fort Sheridan from where they were returned to Germany.

In addition to prisoners, American women entered the workforce in large numbers to fill the voids left by departing servicemen. Women in the workforce was to be just one of the many changes the country would experience on the "home front" during the four long years of World War II.

Homewood schoolchildren and their teachers participate in a war bond rally held in front of the village hall on Chestnut Road.

After the attack on Pearl Harbor, the U.S. economy shifted almost overnight to the production of war-related materials. Manufacturing of consumer goods took a back seat to military production, and rationing of some items was implemented shortly after President Roosevelt's declaration of war. The war required the total commitment and sacrifice of every man, woman, and child, whether soldier or civilian.

Rubber became the first commodity to be rationed after the Japanese invaded the Dutch West Indies and natural supplies were totally cut off. Gasoline rationing reduced the number of miles the average citizen drove, and thus conserved rubber. Voluntary gas rationing proved ineffective, and by the end of 1942, mandatory gas rationing was in effect throughout the country. On average, motorists who used their cars for "nonessential" purposes were restricted to four gallons of gas a week. As the war continued, production of almost every conceivable product was either discontinued or reduced in an effort to divert crucial resources to the war effort.

New car production ceased beginning January 1, 1942, as auto plants converted to manufacturing tanks, planes, and other military vehicles. Other industrial plants quickly retooled their assembly lines for the production of essential defense supplies. By 1944, even whisky disappeared from liquor store shelves as distillers switched to the production of industrial alcohols. By this time, the United States had become the world's largest weapons producer, and management of resources was a tremendous task.

The federal government took on this job and set up the War Production Board and the War Manpower Commission to coordinate the efforts of industry, agriculture, and the military. The Office of Price Administration (OPA) was established to prevent inflation by regulating prices on most commodities. The OPA was also empowered to ration scarce consumer goods and accomplished this by setting up offices in communities throughout the country administered by local appointees. In Homewood, the local price and ration board used an office in the village hall and was headed initially by Stewart Reid and later by E. Austin Rice. The board included members Lawrence Clark, Albert Peloquin, Walter Muszynski, Dr. E. C. Paulsen, and Charles Sublette. These men, who served without pay, were charged with the unenviable task of enforcing the OPA regulations affecting prices and the rationing of a long list of products that grew to include sugar, coffee, meats, processed foods, shoes, and other items of clothing.

The ration board issued a coupon book to every adult and child

Victory Garden catalog of Vaughan's Seed Company. The Vaughan family had a large farm and home on 175th Street west of Calumet Country Club for many years. *(Flossmoor Public Library)*

in the village each month. Rationed goods were assigned a price and point value, and the coupons served to restrict the quantities of particular goods an individual could purchase. Once their coupons were exhausted, people could not buy the rationed goods until the next month. The ration board also heard appeals from families with hardships and granted or rejected requests for additional coupons. Food rationing was the most difficult to acclimate to, and residents were encouraged to plant "victory gardens" to supplement their food stocks. These gardens sprouted in yards all over Homewood and kept everyone in town well fed.

The government also organized the Office of Civilian Defense (OCD). The OCD made good use of civilian patriots who wanted to lend a helping hand defending their country. The OCD prepared disaster and evacuation plans, provided first aid training, and published booklets to help Americans prepare for the possibility the war would invade their own soil. Undertaker Fred Cordt was appointed Civil Defense director in Homewood and was assisted by Fire Chief Nick Kuhn. Cordt recruited volunteers from all across town to serve as air raid wardens and block captains. These people saw to it that their neighbors were trained to act in an emergency. They were issued white helmets, armbands, and a whistle as symbols of their office, and they conducted periodic air raid and blackout drills to test the village's preparedness.

Residents also helped out in other ways. Boy Scouts and other groups collected paper, rubber, and cans and other scrap metals to be recycled for the war effort. Even used cooking fats were deemed an

Homewood Boy Scouts display the result of one of their paper drives during World War II. The photo was taken in front of the American Legion Hall, which stood on Ridge Road at Highland Avenue.

essential defense supply and were collected by grocers nationwide for reuse in munitions production.

Homewood Boy Scouts enjoy a refreshing soda in front of the village auditorium during one of their World War II scrap drives.

Women throughout the country volunteered with the Red Cross to perform a variety of duties, including helping to organize blood drives. Homewood's contingent is shown mustering for a parade at Ridge Road and Dixie Highway during the war.

Hundreds of citizens donated blood in Red Cross blood drives held at the village hall. Villagers also supported the war effort by buying bonds, and their dollar contributions always exceeded the quotas set for the community. School children demonstrated their patriotism by participating in these federal bond and stamp drives too. Students at St. Joseph School were awarded the Treasury Department's Minute Man flag in May 1944 for their exceptional efforts selling over $17,165 in war bonds and stamps. Ninety percent of the children at the school participated in these fundraising efforts by making weekly purchases of stamps or bonds. Money collected by the school was used to buy an army jeep, a field ambulance, and a trainer plane named *Our Lady of Victory*, which included a plate mounted in the cockpit inscribed with the school's name.

Earlier in the war, Homewood women led by Mrs. Harry Shaw donated over five hundred cakes during 1942 to the Servicemen's Center in downtown Chicago. These cakes were served to servicemen as they stopped in Chicago on their way to assignments overseas.

While Homewood had no industrial plants to help churn out armaments or other defense supplies, it did have an airport that figured prominently, training air corps cadets during the war. Washington Park Airport was located on Halsted Street south of 187th Street. The airport was chartered in December 1939 and was managed by Arthur Schweer and Leo Zizic, both of Crete. Before the war, the airport offered flying lessons to novices and hangar storage facilities for airplane owners, and it also provided shuttle services to and from Washington Park Race Track for the many horse race fans who flew in and out of the airfield.

In September 1942, the airport entered into contract with the United States Army and the Civil Aeronautics Authority to provide flight

Father Stephen Sullivan watches members of the American Legion raise the flag at a wartime ceremony in front of St. Joseph School on Dixie Highway.

Washington Park Airport was located on the west side of Halsted Street south of 187th Street.

training to newly recruited cadets. These cadets trained for non-combat duty in the ferry and transport commands and as glider pilots. The eight-week course they were given consisted of 240 hours of ground training and 45 hours of flight instruction. The air cadets were housed in a large cottage on the grounds of the Glenwood Manual Training School across Halsted Street from the airport. The cadets also used a classroom in the school for ground instruction, the school's mess hall for their meals, and the school's parade ground for drills. All flight instruction was provided at the airport by airport instructors. After the war, the "port" returned to offering general civil aviation services, but its future was short-lived. A fire in August 1947 destroyed the airport's south hangar while a second fire in February 1950 destroyed the remaining hangar and an office building on the airport grounds.

After four years, the commitments, sacrifice, and industrial might of the American people paid great dividends when the Germans

Control tower and hangar at Washington Park Airport.

unconditionally surrendered to the Allied powers on May 7, 1945. News of victory in Europe was met with muted celebration in Homewood as townspeople realized only half the war was won, and much work was left to be done to subdue the Japanese.

Reinforcing this cautious mood was the report received of the death of Peter Strine, the last casualty Homewood would suffer in the war. Strine, a paratrooper, had been wounded in the neck prior to V-E Day and died July 12, 1945, while recuperating in a French rest camp. He had lived for many years near the Chicago Military Academy located north of 183rd Street on Leavitt Street, now Perth Avenue. Strine and other neighborhood boys often participated in sports and musical events with academy students, some of whom also went to war and never returned. The academy, a boarding school headed by former military officers, was located in the old Stumer mansion and was established in 1931. A fire damaged the building in August 1939, and the academy never reopened in Homewood.

A month after Strine's death, the day Homewood and the entire world prayed for finally came. On Tuesday, August 14, 1945, President Harry Truman announced the surrender of Japan. The live radio broadcast of Truman's announcement was heard in Homewood at six o'clock that evening. Once the broadcast was finished, a momentary hush fell over the village. Then Homewood, like the rest of the nation, literally went "nuts" and with just cause. Another "war to end all wars" had been won.

Advertisement for the Chicago Military Academy located on Leavitt Street (Perth Avenue) north of 183rd Street. ***(James Daanen)***

Top: **Peter Strine was the last casualty Homewood suffered in World War II.** ***(Margaret Kettren)***

The Homewood fire siren broke the silence and sounded its victory salute, and the siren was soon joined by a cacophony of whistles from rail engines sitting in the Markham Yards. Cars tooting their horns jammed the intersection of Dixie Highway and Ridge Road, and these vehicles joined an impromptu parade that was led by Homewood's two fire engines, their sirens wailing and loaded with average citizens and firemen alike. Young Norm Kranz even drove a tractor from the Homewood Farms Dairy into town; he was so anxious to share in the celebration. Many revelers visited the local taverns in town, and all were well behaved throughout the evening. As a new day dawned, the devout attended services at the village's churches, giving thanks to the Almighty the war had ended and praying life would soon return to normal.

Top: **Cornerstone-laying ceremonies, Memorial Day 1949, for the Wally Burns Memorial Post of the VFW at 18147 Harwood Avenue. Rev. Stephen Sullivan, Rev. C. T. Garriott, Mr. & Mrs. W. A. Burns, Rev. Robert Hollett, and Post Commander Arthur Welsh are pictured.** ***(Peggy Burns)***

Arthur Senior ***(Homewood Izaak Walton)***

Memorial flagpole on the grounds of the Homewood Izaak Walton Preserve ***(Homewood Izaak Walton)***

Although it would take a couple of years, life did return to normal. Like their counterparts after the end of the First World War, returning servicemen interested in maintaining bonds they forged during World War II established the Homewood post of the Veterans of Foreign Wars. The post, named in memory of Walter Burns, Homewood's first war death, was organized August 31, 1946. George Bentley was named the post's first commander while Roy Cofran served as vice commander and William Smith served as junior vice commander.

Earlier in 1946, Homewood resident Arthur Senior persuaded the Illinois Central to donate thirty-three acres of land to the village of Homewood. The land north of Ridge Road and west of Halsted Street had been used by the railroad in the late teens and early twenties to "mine" sand as fill for their track elevation project. Since the railroad project was completed in 1926, the sand pits remained undisturbed and barren.

Senior, a tireless civic booster and member of the Izaak Walton League of America, believed the land and lakes could be reclaimed to serve as a fine recreational amenity for the village. Senior and other men in the community formed a local chapter of the Izaak Walton League and named it Memorial Chapter in honor of the veterans who served in both world wars. After Memorial Chapter received its charter, a lease agreement was signed with the village of Homewood on March 30, 1946, granting stewardship of the thirty-three acres of land to the "Ikes."

Volunteers refurbish the interior and exterior of a former German POW barracks moved to Homewood to become the chapter house at the Izaak Walton Preserve. *(Homewood Izaak Walton)*

Membership in the chapter grew, and work proceeded on improving the land. A memorial garden, envisioned as a living tribute to the veterans, was developed and included a flagpole set amongst evergreens and flowers planted at its base. The Veterans of Foreign Wars donated a spruce tree, and planting was completed in time for a dedication ceremony conducted by Homewood Post 483 of the American Legion on September 8, 1946. Later, the chapter secured an old barracks from the former Civilian Conservation Corps and German POW camp south of Thornton to use for their meetings and activities. The barracks was moved to Homewood in 1947 and remodeled into a clubhouse. The building was aptly named Senior Hall to honor the chapter's founder. Today, the Homewood Izaak Walton Preserve has grown to include 170 acres, and its membership numbers over one thousand.

Shortly after the Izaak Walton Chapter organized, the Bank of Homewood opened in the former quarters of the defunct Homewood State Bank located on the northwest corner of Ridge Road and Martin Avenue. The reestablishment of a bank in Homewood satisfied a definite need for all residents and business owners in town. The bank's officers included A. A. Sommerfield, chairman; jeweler George May who served as president; Dr. Helge Jansen who served as vice president; and Horace Russell, Dr. E. E. Dillon, coal and lumber dealer John Blair, hardware store owner Robert Lewis, and liquor store owner George Alexander, directors.

The year also saw brothers, and former servicemen, Steve and John Surma open their restaurant at the corner of 175th Street and Dixie

Highway in the building formerly occupied by the Amalfi Gardens. The Surmas and their classic American fare of chicken, steaks, and fish were a hit with south suburbanites from the start and for fifty-seven years thereafter! Surma's closed in 2003, ending a remarkable five decades in Homewood. Leona's Restaurant now occupies the building.

Thomas Kataras Sr. and Thomas Bannon also started other businesses in town after the war, which are still operating today. In 1947, Kataras opened the Homewood Sweet Shop in the space formerly occupied by Alexander's Sweet Shop at 1961 Ridge Road. Kataras and his son, Thomas Jr., moved the restaurant to a new building they built at 1944 Ridge Road in 1966. A third generation, led by grandson Tom, continues to operate the restaurant now known as Tom's Family Restaurant in the downtown location. In July 1947, Thomas Bannon started his carpet sales and installation business at 18120 Dixie Highway, which is still run by his son James and his family.

Brothers John and Steve Surma look over the menu in the kitchen of their restaurant at 175th Street and Dixie Highway. *(Don Surma)*

Top:* Interior of the Bank of Homewood shortly after it opened in 1946. *(Great Lakes Bank)

Returning servicemen, many of whom were married during or shortly after the war, were faced with a number of shortages when they returned home. It took time for industry to retool to produce consumer goods to meet the pent-up demands of Americans. Many items remained in short supply for a number of years following the war. One major shortage involved a lack of adequate housing. During the Depression years and throughout the war, there was little construction of new homes and apartment buildings. In Homewood, Ely Chulibrk took advantage of this housing shortage by starting a permanent trailer park. Chulibrk, who owned the Ridgeview Service Station at the corner of Halsted Street and Ridge Road, had rented space behind the station for years to horsemen who parked their travel trailers there during the racing season. To help ease the postwar housing crunch, many young families asked to park trailers there year-round, and with that, Ely's Trailer Park got its start. Chulibrk's daughter Dorothy and her husband Ray Thomas took over the park in 1956 and ran the facility until they retired in 2000 and sold it to new owners.

Surma's Restaurant as it appeared in the mid-1950s.

For most, Ely's Trailer Park was a temporary housing solution. By the end of the decade, new subdivisions were on the drawing boards for land all over Homewood. As the village entered the 1950s, houses were popping up with great speed on land that once sprouted stalks of corn and other crops. Homewood's greatest population boom was well underway.

The Ridgeview Service Station at the southwest corner of Ridge Road and Halsted Street in the late 1940s. The Speedway gas station occupies the site today. *(Dorothy and Ray Thomas)*

Scene of a plane crash on Park Avenue, New Year's Day 1950

CHAPTER 12
Boomtown

The 1950s literally started out with a bang, and exciting times continued throughout the rest of the decade. Shortly after midnight on January 1, 1950, two south suburban aviators engaged in a late night flight around the region. The men, who participated in a great deal of preflight revelry, were flying low over downtown Homewood when their plane began to sputter and lose altitude. Narrowly missing the two water towers located behind the village hall, the plane continued its unplanned descent and crashed between the homes located at 17904 and 17916 Park Avenue. The resulting boom jolted residents on the west side of the Illinois Central tracks from their beds. Investigation revealed the plane had run out of gas just prior to the crash, and the pilot was attempting to return to the Rubikam Airport located at 167th Street and California Avenue. Unfortunately, the pilot and his passenger were both killed in the crash. Miraculously, no one on the ground was injured, and only one of the homes suffered minor damage. Curiosity seekers crowded the area most of New Year's Day trying to catch a glimpse of this unusual scene.

A boom of a different sort—the "baby boom"—characterized the following years of the decade. Following the war, from 1946 through 1964, the birthrate in the United States soared. During this period, over seventy-six million babies were born, and the boom peaked in 1957 when a baby was born every seven seconds! The baby boom, coupled with postwar prosperity, fueled the growth of the middle class. Between 1945 and 1960, the median family income, adjusted for inflation, almost doubled. Most families were now able to afford their own homes. During the 1950s, thirteen million new homes were built in this country, and 85 percent of these were built in the suburbs.

Homewood, like hundreds of towns across the country, grew into one of these suburbs. In 1950, the village's population was 5,863; by the end of the decade, the population increased 225 percent and had grown to 13,371. During the first three years of the decade alone, 4,726 people moved into town. Homes were being completed almost daily in the major subdivisions being constructed by builders all over the village. George Arquilla's Burnside Construction Company was constructing houses in the Southgate subdivision; Nathan Manilow's American Community Builders was working on the Governors Park subdivision while Charles Smith's Consolidated Builders Company was building the Stedhall and Downey Manor subdivisions. Drew Construction was finishing homes in an area called Birchwood Manor between Birch and Willow Roads, east of Dixie Highway.

Typical postwar housing constructed in Homewood in the early 1950s.

Top: **183rd Street looking west to Riegel Road from about Hood Avenue.**

This explosive growth was putting a tremendous strain on all municipal services, and it was difficult for the village and school boards to keep up with the increasing demands posed by the large numbers of new residents. One of the first changes the village board made to deal with this growth was to hire a professional city manager. His job was to coordinate the activities of all village departments and to develop a comprehensive plan to manage the growth that was occurring in the community. No longer were the elected village president and trustees, who had other full-time occupations, able to effectively administer all the activities and employees the village was responsible for, without the assistance of a full-time manager. Alan Webster of

Concordia, Kansas, was hired as the village's first manager, and he started work in August 1953.

Webster's task was not an easy one. The village's infrastructure had not kept pace with growth, and by 1953, water department officials were resorting to periodic sprinkling bans in the summer months to conserve water and to dumping sewage into open ditches and creeks in some areas to relieve overflow at the village's sewage treatment plant. In fact, much of the area west of the Governors Highway was not even served by village sewers. Working to solve these problems was one of Webster's first tasks, and solutions would take time, study, and money. After two years of engineering and review, the village presented a plan to voters that called for the construction of a new and larger sewage treatment plant to replace the one built in 1927 and the completion of new wells and expanded water storage and distribution facilities. Voters approved a $1.6 million bond issue to finance these projects in March 1955, and work started immediately on the $500,000 sewage disposal plant. This plant was located on the site of the old facility on 191st Street east of Center Avenue. Work also progressed on over eight miles of new water mains, a new well, and a 500,000-gallon elevated water storage tank located on the west side of town on Rockwell Avenue. By the end of the decade, the village waterworks had expanded to consist of seven wells, four elevated storage tanks with a combined storage capacity of 1,330,000 gallons, and three softening plants. Continued growth, however, still taxed these resources.

Street scene looking west on Ridge Road from Dixie Highway.

Top: **Street scene looking north on Dixie Highway from Ridge Road.**

Completion of new subdivisions also added more streets that had to be swept, patched, and plowed. By 1956, the village had 47 miles of streets, 6.5 miles of which were still rock, cinder, or dirt. During that year, the village bought equipment and started a new program spreading salt at critical intersections and on highly traveled roads during snow and ice storms. Before this, cinders and sand were used with little effect. The street department also supervised the installation of stop and go lights at the intersection of 183rd Street and Dixie Highway in 1955. This intersection was only the second in town to be equipped with automatic controls. In the older areas of town, the street department had to cope with the spread of Dutch elm disease, which decimated the village's population of the stately tree during the decade. At one time, over 3,785 elms graced the village's parkways. Today, fewer than 100 American elms remain.

Improving police and fire protection was another task the village undertook during the decade. In 1950, the police department consisted of Chief Walter Gleason, Sergeant Fred Nyquist, and three patrolmen. Gleason was seventy-two years old and had been with the force since 1904. Nyquist was sixty-seven years old and had been on the force for twenty-five years. Both men retired in 1951, and Mel Meyer, a decorated World War II aviator and a one-year veteran on the force, took over the helm as chief. Under Meyer's leadership, the department grew to include two sergeants, seven patrolmen, and three clerk-dispatchers by 1959. After assuming command, Meyer required officers to take Red Cross first aid training, and the department replaced its sedan patrol cars with station wagons equipped with stretchers that could be used to transport sick and injured in emergencies. Meyer also instituted more effective speed enforcement when the village purchased its first radar-timing device in 1955. That year saw the department's squad cars logging 86,833 miles on patrol.

Sergeant Rudy Meyer, Chief Mel Meyer, and Officer Herbert Meyer stand with new police cars in the late 1950s.

Perhaps the most important improvement in the police department during the decade was the addition of a two-way radio installed in the police station in 1957. Prior to this, when calls were received at the Homewood station, police personnel phoned pertinent information to the Cook County Sheriff's office on Ridge Road. Operators there then transmitted messages over the county radio frequency, which was monitored by the Homewood patrol cars. Cook County had been dispatching Homewood police since the department began operating two-way radios in its squad cars in 1940. In 1936, the department's cars were first equipped with a radio receiver that was tuned to a local commercial broadcast station, which would interrupt its regular programming to beam calls to the Homewood squads. While this method was inefficient, particularly when officers were out of their cars, it was a vast improvement over the method the department had used since the village's first water tower was constructed in 1911. At that time, a red light was placed atop the tower, and when a call needed an officer's attention, the phone operator switched the light on. While on patrol, officers kept an eye on the tower, and when they saw the light on, they phoned the telephone operator to get the information needed to respond to the call for service. This signaling system was discontinued in 1940 when Homewood patrol cars were first equipped with two-way radios.

Homewood police clerks were also responsible for dispatching the fire department. During the 1950s, the Homewood Fire Department continued to be an all-volunteer force. The volunteers were alerted to calls by a siren that was located on top of the village hall. By the mid-1950s, the department also utilized a phone conferencing system called the Galena System that aided the dispatcher in notifying the volunteers of fire calls. When a special phone was picked up at the police station, the phones in all of the firefighters' homes would ring while the dispatcher kept repeating the address and nature of the call. This system was a great improvement as the Homewood village limits expanded and some volunteers lived out of range of the sound of the fire siren.

The fire department's apparatus leaves its quarters in the late 1950s.

Like the police department, the fire department also improved its training and equipment during the decade. Two new pumpers were added to the department's roster in the 1950s, one in 1951 and the other in 1957. Another major change occurred in 1955 when Nick Kuhn, the department's chief since 1930 and a member of the department since 1918, retired. Chief Kuhn, who retired at the age of seventy-nine, was replaced by Thomas White, a department member since 1920. White also ran a floral shop in Homewood.

Village services were not the only ones impacted by growth during the baby boom years. Homewood schools were also severely affected during this time. Enrollment in School District 153 approached 900 students for the 1950–51 school year when students were attending classes in Standard School, Central School, and the newly completed Ridge School located at the southeast corner of Ridge Road and

Ridge School, built on the southeast corner of Ridge Road and Gottschalk Avenue, in 1949

Gottschalk Avenue. Ridge School opened in September 1949 and contained ten classrooms, which helped alleviate overcrowding at the district's two other schools. By 1953, the influx of new families and the large numbers of children continued to tax the district's capacity, and the school board started plans for a new school on Willow Road at Highland Avenue. Willow School was completed in 1953, and an addition to it was built in 1955, bringing the total number of classrooms at this school to twenty-one. Willow School also housed the district's administrative offices, which were under the direction of Elmer Schultz who had assumed the superintendent's position in 1950, a post he held for the next twenty-five years. At the time Willow was being built, the school board also bought twelve acres of land at 183rd Street and Aberdeen Road for the eventual needs of students in this area. A new school was built on this site, which opened in 1957. This school was named in honor of James Hart, one of Homewood's early settlers and a strong proponent of education. James Hart School housed junior high students, and two additions were completed to this facility during the first decade after it opened, one in 1959 and the other in 1963. By 1959, enrollment in all Homewood public schools topped 1,650 students.

In addition to School District 153, School District 161, which served students living west of Governors Highway, and Homewood's parochial schools also experienced rapid growth during the decade. By 1959, St. Joseph School's enrollment had grown to over one thousand students. The school was enlarged in 1942, 1951, and 1955, and by the end of the decade, it held twenty-four classrooms and a gymnasium. At this same time, Salem Lutheran School had an enrollment of about fifty students. The parochial schools not only served the religious and educational needs of their congregation's children, they also helped relieve the tax burden in town. Taxes to support the public schools would have increased significantly if even small numbers of parochial students attended the public schools.

As the numbers of school-age children increased in Homewood and neighboring Flossmoor, residents of these communities became interested in the proposition of a local high school to serve both towns.

Depending on where students lived, they either attended Thornton, Bloom, or Bremen Township High Schools. Many parents felt the increasing enrollments in the elementary schools in each town and the forecasts of future growth for the two villages made it practical for establishing a community high school. A local high school would also reduce the distance and time it took for students to travel to and from school, and it would foster greater community spirit.

In early 1954, a small group known as the Citizens for a Homewood-Flossmoor High School conducted a study on the feasibility of creating a new high school district. The group elicited and received the support of both the Homewood and Flossmoor PTAs, and on September 30, a public meeting was held in the Homewood village auditorium that was attended by over five hundred residents. A majority of those present expressed enthusiasm for the proposal, and a petition drive was started to obtain the necessary signatures requesting permission from the Cook County Board of School Trustees to allow detachment from the existing districts and the creation of a new high school district. Signatures of two-thirds of all eligible Homewood and Flossmoor voters were required, and within two weeks, the group had obtained the signatures of 5,971 names. Petitions were submitted to the Cook County Board for approval on October 15. At a subsequent hearing held in the offices of the Cook County Superintendent of Schools, opposing figures were presented to show that the petitions did not bear the necessary two-thirds majority. This position was upheld, and the petitions were withdrawn.

Conceptual rendering of Homewood-Flossmoor Community High School, which opened in September 1959

Undaunted by this setback, the group persevered with greater vigor. During 1955, the League of Women Voters in Homewood and Flossmoor voted to study further the feasibility of establishing a high school. Public fact-finding meetings were held, and a professional survey prepared by the University of Illinois was distributed to all households. On July 19, a representative of the university presented a report favorable to the high school proposition, and the League and other community organizations lent their support. With this, a second petition drive was started, and by December, 8,060 signatures were gathered and submitted to the county board. A team of Bureau of Census statisticians verified accuracy of the petitions, and in February 1957, the county board rendered a favorable decision allowing a new district to be established.

Homewood-Flossmoor High School District 233 became an official reality on July 1, 1957. Following this, bonds were issued to purchase eighty acres on Flossmoor Road between Governors Highway and Kedzie Avenue, and a building containing fifty-one classrooms capable of accommodating fifteen hundred students was constructed. H-F High School opened its doors in September 1959 with an enrollment of 987 students and a staff of 59 teachers under the direction of Dr. William O. Woodworth, the school's superintendent.

Homewood's park board was another governmental agency that was affected by the growth of the baby boom years. The park board was organized as an independent government body in 1947, and George Day served as the board's first president. At this time, the board assumed control of Merchant's Park, the land that was formerly occupied by Gottschalk's Pavilion. The pavilion had fallen into disrepair and was torn down in the early 1940s. The property was then acquired by a group of local businessmen who donated it to the village for a park with the only stipulation that the village recognize their donation—thus the name Merchant's Park. The Homewood Racquet Club, a group of local tennis enthusiasts, assisted the village improving the site with tennis courts. Playground equipment, picnic facilities, and a baseball diamond that could be flooded for skating in the winter rounded out the park's amenities.

Dr. Karl Schmidt *(Field Museum)*

The village's second park was a one-half-acre lot donated to the park board by Dr. Karl Schmidt. The lot on Cedar Road at Highland Avenue had been vacant since the house built on the site was destroyed by fire in 1933. The park contained playground equipment for young children and at one time boasted the largest sandbox in Cook County. Schmidt, an internationally renowned zoologist, was curator emeritus of the Field Museum of Natural History and lived at 1751 Cedar Road. One of Schmidt's areas of expertise was the study of snakes, and he frequently wrote books and gave lectures in which he tried to allay people's fears of snakes and snakebites.

Ironically, it was a snakebite that led to Dr. Schmidt's death. While assisting other colleagues, including Dr. Robert Inger, also of Homewood and curator of reptiles at the museum, examine and identify a 30" South African tree snake for the Lincoln Park Zoo, Dr. Schmidt was bitten in the left thumb. At first, Dr. Schmidt appeared to have had only a slight reaction to the bite, but he subsequently took ill while riding an I.C. train back to Homewood. The following day, September 26, 1957, Schmidt felt better in the morning and had planned on returning to the museum. By midafternoon, however, he collapsed in his home and was taken to Ingalls Hospital where he died of massive hemorrhaging and respiratory collapse. The snake was later identified as a poisonous Boomslang. Schmidt, the consummate scientist, kept a detailed diary during the last hours of his illness, which described the symptoms of the venomous bite step-by-step as they developed. Many of Schmidt's books are still in print today, and his diary entries were helpful in developing bite treatments and antidotes.

By the end of the decade, Homewood had developed additional parkland, much of which was acquired through subdivision requirements placed on developers. The village's parks then were Hillcrest Park located in Governors Park between Spruce and Locust Roads; Briarwood Park (now Willowview) adjacent to Willow School; Ashland Park (now Indian Trails) located at Willow Road and Ashland Avenue; and Orchard Park on Olive Road, which contained a baseball diamond that was used by Homewood Little League and Pony League teams in addition to the fields the league, which was organized in 1951, maintained at the Izaak Walton Preserve.

Homewood's service clubs like the Rotary, Legion, Lions, and Kiwanis were early sponsors of Homewood Little League, organized in 1951.

Homewood's most popular recreational venue and its first public pool opened in 1957. Lions Club pool was financed and built by the Homewood-Flossmoor Lions Club Community Service Corporation on land in the 1000 block of Ridge Road that was once part of the Mackenzie Farm. The pool, which initially measured 75' x 82' has been enlarged several times over the years and is now part of the park system.

Lions Club pool, completed in 1957, has been significantly expanded over the years.

Church membership also burgeoned in the baby boom years. During the 1950s, each of the village's four established congregations built new sanctuaries to accommodate the growth in their membership. St. Joseph's Church,

under the leadership of its pastor Rev. Stephen Sullivan and associate pastor Rev. Joseph Burke, embarked on an ambitious building program in 1954. Construction was completed on a convent to house the nuns who taught at St. Joseph School, and construction also started that year on the parish's new church building. The new church was built just south of the original structure where services were held until dedication ceremonies took place for the new building on April 24, 1955. Following this, the old church was torn down to make way for a rectory to house the parish priests. Father Sullivan, a colorful and beloved figure in the community for thirty years, retired in June 1955 after which Father Burke was appointed pastor.

St. Joseph School, Rectory, Church, and Convent as they looked after the church was completed in 1955.

Salem Lutheran Church on Ashland Avenue was completed in 1956.

Salem Lutheran Church was the next congregation to act to solve the overcrowding at its Sunday services. Flanked on the south by a brick schoolhouse and on the north by a parsonage, there was no room on Morris Avenue to expand Salem's little white church. In 1954, land was purchased on Ashland Avenue south of 183rd Street for the site of a new building. Groundbreaking took place in November 1954, and a new $160,000 church was dedicated in ceremonies held March 11, 1956, under the direction of Pastor Walther Wilk. A parsonage and a new school were also completed on this site in 1964.

St. Paul Church also began plans for enlarging its facilities in 1954. After considering various options, the congregation elected to proceed with a $215,000 plan, which called for the construction of a new sanctuary on the south side of their property. The new sanctuary was connected to the old church by a wing housing offices, meeting rooms, and classrooms. The old frame sanctuary was preserved and covered with face brick to match the style of the new building. Before work could proceed, the old German schoolhouse, built on the property in 1862, was torn down, and the parsonage was moved to a lot on Martin Avenue. Construction commenced in 1955, and the Rev. Dr. Christopher Garriott and members of St. Paul's dedicated their new building in ceremonies held on March 17, 1956. In keeping with tradition, the church's bell, which was such an integral part of Homewood's early years, was proudly reinstalled in a belfry above the new sanctuary where it remains to this day.

Homewood's oldest congregation, the First Presbyterian Church, erected a new building north of their existing church on Gottschalk Avenue in 1957–58. The beautiful Georgian Colonial-style structure was dedicated in services held on December 7, 1958. The ceremonies, led by Rev. Robert Hollett, the church's pastor since 1945, also coincided with the culmination of the church's centennial year.

St. Paul's new sanctuary under construction in 1955. *(St. Paul Community Church)*

The decade also saw the establishment of five new churches in town to meet the religious needs of Homewood's growing population. Faith Lutheran Church was organized in 1951, and their first services were held in the VFW Hall on Harwood Avenue on December 9. Services were later held in the American Legion Hall on Ridge Road and in the Homewood Village Hall. Rev. Clifton Kettelson was named Faith's first pastor. In 1952, the congregation purchased the land on Dixie Highway at 186th Place, formerly owned by the C. A. Baker family. The old farmhouse on the property was used as a parsonage, and groundbreaking for a church building was held September 27, 1953. The church was dedicated on May 23, 1954. The congregation grew quickly, and a new and larger sanctuary, the current church, was completed in 1964.

Members of the Homewood Reformed Church celebrated their first worship services in the Homewood Village Hall under the direction of the Rev. Herman J. Ridder on July 6, 1952. The congregation had purchased several lots at

Artist rendering of the new First Presbyterian Church completed in 1958.

Willow Road and Highland Avenue on which construction of a church building took place. Dedication services for the new church were held on December 5, 1952. The congregation quickly outgrew this building on Highland Avenue, and a new sanctuary was built on Willow Road and dedicated April 19, 1959. Homewood Reformed Church changed its name in 1999 to the Living Springs Community Church, and in 2002, construction of a new building was completed on Halsted Street in Glenwood. The church property in Homewood was then sold to School District 153, which demolished the buildings to make room for a parking lot.

Another congregation officially organized in 1952 was the Homewood Baptist Church, which was chartered by the Baptist General Conference of America on May 15 of that year. Members of the congregation, however, had been holding services in the Homewood Village Hall since July 1951, and the group subsequently used the American Legion Hall when more room was needed. The church, under the direction of its pastor Rev. James Merrill Smith, began construction of a new building at 183rd Street and Governors Highway in June 1955. Dedication services for this edifice were held on September 16, 1956.

Faith Lutheran, Homewood Reformed, and Homewood Baptist were other Homewood churches that completed new buildings during the 1950s.

After an absence of over thirty years, a group of Christian Scientists began holding Sunday morning services and Sunday school exercises in the Homewood Theatre in September 1952. The Christian Scientists later held Sunday services and Wednesday evening meetings at the Homewood Village Hall, James Hart School, and finally at the old telephone exchange at 1853 Ridge Road until a church building was built in the 1300 block of 183rd

Street in 1965. This building was sold in 2001 and now houses the South Suburban Church of God.

By the end of the decade, Homewood also had a church to serve those of the Methodist denomination. Plans for St. Andrew's United Methodist Church were started in 1957, and services were first held in the Homewood Village Hall on November 11. The church was officially chartered on February 23, 1958, and the Rev. Virgil Chilcote assumed pastoral duties in July. The church also purchased land at Idlewild and Riegel Roads in 1958 although a new church building was not completed on the property until October 1962.

Business also flourished in Homewood during the decade. The growth in the new subdivisions put a strain on existing stores downtown. Neighborhood shopping centers opened up on the outskirts of the village to cater to the new families moving into town. Southgate on Dixie Highway was the first of these "centers" to open. Built in 1951, Southgate Shopping Center was anchored by Garofalo's Finer Foods, Jack's Liquors, Zeek's Hardware Store, the Neighborhood Cleaners, C. A. Baker's Realty office, and Carter's (later Southgate) Pharmacy. Westgate Shopping Center on 183rd Street at Western Avenue was built in 1955, and Kingston Cleaners and Homewood Glass and Mirror were two of the stores to open in this plaza. Both are still in business today. On the north side of town, construction on the Northgate Shopping Center on Dixie Highway south of 175th Street started in 1959. When completed in 1960, the Convenient Food Mart and Jacobson's Drugs were two of the first tenants.

Southgate Shopping Center as it appeared in the late 1950s

New stores also populated the downtown business district. The old Zimmer home that stood on the southwest corner of Ridge Road and Martin Avenue was torn down in 1955, and the Ridge-Mar Shopping Center was built in its place. The new building housed

Ridge-Mar Shopping Center, at the southwest corner of Ridge Road and Martin Avenue, built in 1955

Aurelio's Pizza as it appears today. ***(Clay Denton)***

Top: **Joe Aurelio mans the pizza oven at his first restaurant on Ridge Road.** ***(Aurelio's Pizza)***

the Melody Mart, the Toy Box, The Shoe Horn, Brainerd Men's Wear, Dutch Mill Candies, Schreiber's Hardware, and B & R Pizza when it first opened.

By 1959, Joe Aurelio, at the age of twenty-six, opened his first pizzeria in this building with $1,500 down and one employee. The restaurant seated sixteen people, and business started slowly at first. By 1962, business had grown to the extent that Aurelio expanded into an adjacent storefront where seating capacity grew to eighty and his roster of employees grew to fifteen. Business continued to boom, and several additional expansions followed in the late 1960s. By the end of the decade, the restaurant had a seating capacity of two hundred and was employing over fifty people. Customers were coming from all over the south suburbs and as far as Chicago, Joliet, and northwest Indiana to have an Aurelio's Pizza.

Growth continued in the 1970s, and a separate carryout location was opened on Ridge Road east of Martin Avenue in 1972. Joe Aurelio opened his first franchise in 1975, and a year later, he purchased the old 15,000-square-foot Kurtz building at 18162 Harwood Avenue, with a dream of remodeling it into what would be billed as the world's largest pizzeria. After a year of construction and an investment of close to $1 million, Aurelio's dream came true, and his new restaurant, with the capacity to seat six hundred customers, opened on December 6, 1977. Today, Aurelio's Pizza is a true Homewood success story and has grown substantially over the years to a total of forty locations in seven states. Recognized for its commitment to quality and community, Aurelio's ranks in the top one hundred pizza franchises in the country and in the top ten in all Chicagoland.

During the decade, supermarkets like the Kroger's and Jewel Tea stores on Dixie Highway and a new A & P store on 183rd Street were replacing the small storefront grocers downtown. Homewood also saw its first fast food restaurants when Dog 'n Suds and Burger Chef both opened "drive-ins" on Dixie Highway. Burger Chef, located across from

Surma's, and the Dog 'n Suds, located a block north of 183rd Street, were popular "hangouts" for teenagers from throughout the area.

The Dog 'n Suds was built on the property that formerly was the home of August John Mueller. Mueller, born in 1874, earned international fame as the "Thomas Edison of roller coasters." Known professionally as "John A. Miller," Mueller traveled throughout the United States and Mexico designing and supervising the construction of roller coasters and other amusement rides. Mueller was also a gifted inventor, and many of his inventions increased coaster safety. When not on a jobsite, Mueller would return to Homewood and continue his design work in the office on the second floor of his home on Miller Court. The house was moved to allow for the construction of the Dog 'n Suds.

East side of the 18200 block of Dixie Highway looking toward 183rd Street in the late 1950s.

Across from the Dog 'n Suds, the Illinois Bell Telephone Company completed construction of a modern telephone exchange building in 1957. The old Doepp and Scupham home that occupied this site was moved a lot to the west on Martin Avenue. Equipment in the new building allowed for direct dial service of all local calls, which eliminated the need for large numbers of telephone operators who had previously placed these calls manually for telephone customers. The equipment was placed in service on October 20, 1957. Direct dialing of long distance calls followed shortly thereafter. At this time, Homewood telephone numbers were assigned the "SYcamore" 8 and 9 prefixes.

Ridge Road looking east toward Dixie Highway from Harwood Avenue in the late 1950s.

Other businesses opened during the decade, and many are still operating today. Hoekstra Heating Company, Florence Draperies, Wilson's Rental, and the Rickshaw Chinese Restaurant are a few by name.

Modern shopping centers, improved village services, larger schools, and new parks and churches all served as part of the foundation to make Homewood an attractive place to live and work. Because of these amenities, the postwar boom that began in the 1950s continued unabated in Homewood throughout the next decade. Despite the prosperity at home, however, the era was also characterized by troubles around the world.

Nike missile is raised for inspection. The Nike missile base in Homewood was located in the 19000 block of Halsted Street and was constructed in 1954–55. *(Adam Russell)*

CHAPTER 13
Boomtown, Part 2

The postwar years were also tumultuous ones marked by uncertainty and tension around the globe. After the war, the United States and the Union of the Soviet Socialist Republics (USSR) emerged as the world's major powers. Although both countries were allied during the war, they espoused different ideologies. This led to a deteriorating relationship between them after the war. The Soviets backed the installation of communist regimes throughout Eastern Europe, which infuriated the United States and threatened the democratic principles the U.S. had fought for. Hostility developed between the countries, and they teetered on the edge of direct military action. In addition, the USSR signed an alliance with the People's Republic of China, and communism spread to areas outside of Europe. These developments combined to create a heightened state of affairs known as the Cold War, which lasted from the mid-1940s through the end of the 1980s.

Early on, Chinese-backed communist forces from North Korea invaded South Korea, and the United States led United Nations forces intervening in this conflict. After three years of bitter fighting, the Korean War ended in 1953. Two young soldiers from Homewood, George Eustis and James Morrison, were killed in Korean battles.

In 1950, the United States also offered assistance to France in the form of military advisers and financial support to save French Indochina, now Vietnam, from communist rule. After the French withdrew from the country in 1954, the United States backed the South Vietnamese government, and friction with North Vietnam continued, ultimately breaking out into a full-fledged war in 1959. The United States sent troops to fight alongside the South Vietnamese in 1965. A long and bloody engagement, the Vietnam War continued until 1975 when Saigon eventually fell to the Communists. The war claimed the lives of eleven men from Homewood and Flossmoor. Gary Barnard, Phillip Zummallen, William Cofran, Paul Severson, William Oskilanec, Thomas McGrath, James Ward, Bruce Peterson, Phillip Flannigan, Park Bunker, and Jeffrey Lemon were those from Homewood and Flossmoor killed in Vietnam and neighboring Laos between the years of 1966 and 1971.

The Cold War also led to a dramatic escalation in the development of and the numbers of conventional and nuclear warheads. Soviet arms buildup and expansionist tendencies led the United States to develop defensive missile systems to protect the country. In 1953, the United States Army began building the Nike Missile Defense System to protect American cities and military and industrial installations from the threat of attack from Soviet aircraft.

Nike, named after the Greek goddess of victory, was the nation's first guided surface-to-air missile and included computer and radar elements to ensure accuracy. At the system's peak in the early 1960s, there were three hundred missile batteries protecting over forty cities around the country. Twenty-three of these, including facilities in Homewood, ringed the city of Chicago and the Gary steel mills.

Construction of the Homewood Nike missile base commenced in the fall of 1954 on cornfields in the southeast section of town. Located in the 19000 block of Halsted Street, three large underground concrete reinforced vaults were built to house the missiles and their launching platforms. Unless the missiles were raised, no trace of these bunkers or their contents would normally be visible. When completed in the summer of 1955, eighteen Ajax missiles were installed at this base. Six of these first-generation Nike missiles were installed in each pit and carried a conventional warhead capable of destroying a single aircraft. Second-generation Nike Hercules missiles were installed at the Homewood facility in 1959. Each vault was equipped with four of these nuclear warheads, which could target several aircraft at once. Third-generation Nike Zeus missiles were never placed in Homewood.

One-half mile to the north on 187th Street, the site of Patriot's Park today, the Army constructed a companion radar facility, which could not only detect incoming foreign aircraft but would also track the missiles once fired. This base included five radar platforms that were enclosed in large and distinctive white spheres shaped like golf balls. The radar site also included the headquarters and administrative offices, barracks, and mess hall for both facilities. A tennis court

rounded out the amenities at this location.

After construction was completed, ninety-two officers and enlisted men of the United States Army's Twenty-second Antiaircraft Group staffed the Nike units in Homewood. In 1963, civilian reservists took over operations and manned the missile and radar facilities until they were deactivated in 1974. Days were filled with maintenance, repairs, training, and drills. Radar had to be monitored, and security was always tight, day and night. At the missile site, guard dogs patrolled the grounds after dark. The facilities were staffed around the clock although many technicians and administrative personnel worked day shifts and were on call at night if needed.

The Nike missile radar base was located on the north side of 187th Street west of Center Avenue. The facility was deactivated in 1974, and the site is now Patriot's Park. ***(Adam Russell)***

Aerial view of the Nike radar base just prior to deactivation of the facility in 1974. ***(Chicago Heights Library)***

In October 1962, all personnel were on duty after the United States confirmed that the Soviet Union had begun to construct nuclear missile bases in Cuba. These bases were being constructed to house both medium-range and intermediate-range ballistic missiles, the latter of which were capable of reaching targets up to 2200 nautical miles. These missiles placed most major U.S. cities—including New York, Chicago, and Los Angeles—within range of nuclear attack. On October 22, President Kennedy made this discovery public. Kennedy also ordered a "quarantine" around Cuba, which blocked any further Soviet ships from reaching the island nation, and he demanded the removal of the missiles already there. If ignored, Kennedy warned that there would be "a full retaliatory response upon the Soviet Union."

During thirteen days in October 1962, October 16–28, the world came as close as anytime before or since to the brink of nuclear war. During this period, now known as the Cuban Missile Crisis, soldiers at Homewood's Nike base were on the highest state of alert, and the twelve Nike missiles found there were "hot"—pointed skyward and ready to be fired—for three full days. This was the only time in the base's existence that the missiles were raised for a real threat.

After the Cuban crisis, the Soviets developed intercontinental ballistic missiles (ICBMs), and the Nike system was incapable of dealing with this threat. Nike was intended to deal with invading aircraft, and the new Soviet weapons rendered the Nike bases less critical to the nation's defense. By the mid-1960s, the Army began to close these facilities throughout the country. The Strategic Arms Limitation Treaty (SALT), signed in 1972, included the removal of the remaining Nike missiles. By 1974, all Nike batteries, including Homewood's, were phased out with the exception of four batteries in Florida and Alaska. In the end, not a single missile was ever fired from a Nike installation.

Aerial view of downtown Homewood in 1974 *(Chicago Heights Library)*

Following deactivation of the facilities in Homewood, Reserve units used the buildings and grounds at the radar base through 1984. That year, a new building was built for these units at the former missile base on Halsted Street, and Illinois National Guard units then occupied the 187th Street buildings until they were finally abandoned in 1990. For the next decade, the land and buildings on 187th Street remained vacant until the federal government gave them to the Homewood-Flossmoor Park District. All buildings on the site were demolished, and construction of a beautiful park, appropriately named Patriot's Park, was completed in 2002.

Despite the chill of the Cold War, life went on normally in Homewood. Normal meant continued growth in the village's population and development of the town's remaining farmland. In 1960, Homewood's population was 13,371; in 1970 it hit 18,871; and by 1980, the population had risen to 19,724. During this time, the Riegel Manor, Homewood Terrace, and Woodborough subdivisions were completed on the east side of town, and the Dolphin Lake and Homewood Estates subdivisions were finished on the west side of town. Riegel Manor, located east of Riegel Road and north of 187th Street, was built on land once farmed by the pioneer Riegel family while the Homewood Terrace subdivision, south of 187th Street and east of Riegel Road, was once the farm of the Meyer family. The Woodborough subdivision, located north of 187th Street and east of Center Avenue, was built on land earmarked at one time for a possible east campus of Homewood-Flossmoor High School. Dolphin Lake and the Homewood Estates subdivisions were developed through the 1970s on land formerly tilled by the Hassbergs and Ehlers.

In addition to subdivisions, new apartment and condominium complexes were also being built in Homewood. Cherry Creek Towers on the west side, Homewood Shores on the east side, and Flosswood Condominiums near the center of town were just a few by name. Flosswood Condos on 183rd Street just west of the Illinois Central tracks was symbolic of how the old made way for the new in the 1960s and 1970s. The condominium buildings were built on the land that had been the site of the old Homewood brickyard and had been abandoned in the 1960s by the Homewood Coal, Ice and Material Company. Downtown on Ridge Road, other landmarks were being given a facelift or torn down altogether in the name of modernization. Mueller's Tavern, on the northeast corner of Ridge and Harwood, with its distinctive corner turret, underwent extensive remodeling in 1965. The turret and the complete second floor of the build-

Flosswood Condominiums on 183rd Street were built on the land that once was the Homewood brickyard.

Mueller's Tavern underwent extensive remodeling in 1965, which included the removal of its second floor and turret, to produce this office building.

ing were torn off, the exterior brick walls were covered with stucco, an addition was built on the east side, and the building was converted to use as offices. Sadly, the "modernized" structure bore no resemblance to the landmark it once was.

Across the street, the Ridgewood Tap building, built in 1896, and the Funk's Hall building, built in 1911, also underwent modernization of their exterior façades. When first built, the Ridgewood building was of frame construction with wood clapboard siding, and the main floor of the building was several feet above street level. To eliminate stairs to the entrance, owner Henry Funk had the building lowered to sidewalk level in 1934. To accomplish this feat, workers had to remove courses of foundation brick, and a deeper basement had to be dug. Funk also had the exterior faced with brick at this time. By the early 1970s, this older brick façade was removed, and the Ridgewood and the neighboring Funk's Hall building were refaced with new brick to achieve a more modern look. Down the street, on the north side of Ridge Road, the Bank of Homewood purchased several buildings west and north of its facility so the bank could build an addition and a larger parking lot. Demolished in this project was the old Zimmer Store, dating to 1855 and more recently occupied as Helen's Dress Shop in the 1950s and 1960s.

Ridge Road looking west from Dixie Highway in the mid-1970s.

The Bank of Homewood after undergoing extensive remodeling in 1974.

On Dixie Highway, the disappearance of several more buildings helped to further transform the downtown business district to give it a more modern look. Near the intersection of Harwood Avenue, the old library had been "bulging at the seams" for years. Library officials attempted to have a new building built in 1958, but voters rejected a referendum proposal that year asking for the funds to do so. By 1961, the dramatic increase in books circulated and patronage at the library,

made it apparent that larger quarters were a necessity. A new library was completed at 17900 Dixie Highway in January 1962, and once all the books were moved from the old library next door, that building was torn down. The old library had served the citizens of Homewood for over 108 years, the first seven decades of which were as the village's train station.

Overcrowding in the police and fire stations led to a referendum to build new facilities for these departments. Construction started in 1966 and was completed in 1968.

A block south of the library on Dixie Highway, the village purchased several lots north of the village hall to provide room for a new public safety building and an expanded parking lot. By the early 1960s, the village hall had become cramped and overcrowded with the increasing number of employees working there. In the police department alone, there were four employees on the payroll when the village hall was first built, but by 1960, that number had swelled to thirteen. In the fire department, the garage to house their apparatus was built to accommodate two trucks, but by 1960, five trucks were packed in this space. Clearly, these two departments needed more room to operate efficiently. After an intensive public information campaign, voters approved an $803,000 bond issue to finance the construction of new police and fire facilities in November 1965. To save money, village firefighters spent a weekend in August 1966 burning down seven buildings along Dixie Highway and Elm Road to clear ground for construction of the Public Safety building. Included in this number were Severson's Garage and the apartment building Andrew Severson built in 1915 by remodeling the original First Presbyterian Church building, which was initially erected around 1859. The village's first water tank tower was also demolished as part of this construction project.

Groundbreaking for the building took place in September 1966, and construction was halted for weeks in late January and early February 1967 after 23 inches of snow fell in Homewood on January 26 and 27. The snowstorm, the worst in Chicago history, crippled the area for days. The blizzard started at about 5:00 A.M. on Thursday the twenty-sixth, and snowfall continued for about thirty-six hours, ending during the early evening on Friday the twenty-seventh. Accompanied by winds of up to fifty miles per hour, the storm whipped snow into drifts four to ten feet high in areas. Realizing the strength of the storm, public works officials made arrangements early on with Alpha Construction Company to borrow several bulldozers and road graders to augment the four village-owned plows in snow removal operations. Even with this help, the blizzard had the upper hand, and traffic ground to a standstill. Many children were forced to spend the night at their schools, and a number of out-of-town motorists stranded on village streets were given accommodations at the village auditorium until the roads were cleared. It wasn't until Monday, January 30, that all streets were plowed to at least one passable lane.

Fortunately, little criminal activity took place during this period, and Police Chief Mel Meyer and Lieutenant Richard Bielfeldt took turns personally operating a bulldozer on loan from Washington Park Race Track to help clear the snow. Firefighters were also on high alert during this time, and the only major incident they had to deal with was a barn fire at Washington Park Race Track. Like a guest who doesn't know when to leave, remnants of the snow did not completely melt for months.

Homewood's Public Safety building after completion in 1968.

Parade heads north on Dixie Highway at 183rd Street in October 1971.

Despite this delay, the new police and fire headquarters were completed in January 1968, and dedication ceremonies took place on May 30 to coincide with Homewood's Diamond Jubilee (seventy-fifth anniversary) celebration.

Farther south on Dixie Highway at 183rd Street, two longtime landmark homes also made way for more commercial development. On the northwest corner of the intersection, the Rosenstein house was moved to Martin Avenue to allow for the construction of a Gulf gasoline station. By 1974, this station was torn down, and Cal's Roast Beef

View looking north on Dixie Highway from 183rd Street in 1976.

Restaurant was built in its place. Today, the site is home to Caribou Coffee and the Hollywood Video store. Across the alley to the north on Dixie Highway, the old Bramstedt home was burned down in 1965 to clear the way for the construction of the Tews Funeral Home. With the demise of these two homes, Dixie Highway was now a completely commercial district from the north Illinois Central viaduct through to 183rd Street.

Many other older homes and buildings were torn down or burned in fire department training exercises during this era, which helped complete the metamorphosis, for better or worse, of Homewood's downtown area into a modern business district.

Above all, however, the demolition of the Standard School on Dixie Highway was an act that was met by more than a tinge of regret for generations of Homewood residents who had attended classes there. Since Standard was built in 1904, thousands of children passed through its doors, and the building was filled with many fond memories. After Churchill School was completed in 1965 near the corner of 190th Street and Center Avenue, Standard's classroom space was no longer needed. Although school enrollment reached 3,036 pupils in 1968, additions to Churchill and those completed earlier to the remaining schools provided sufficient space to adequately accommodate all students. As costs increased to maintain Standard, the school board made plans to demolish the building and sell the land. The school's unceremonious date with the wrecker's ball occurred in December 1970. After that, the north half of the parcel was sold to the village, and the land was used as part of its plans to widen Hickory Road from Harwood Avenue to Dixie Highway. The south part of the parcel was later sold to the park district, and

Standard School, a fixture on Dixie Highway since 1904, was demolished in 1970.

Independence Park, dedicated in July 1976, was built on land once occupied by Standard School. ***(Homewood-Flossmoor Park District)***

Dolphin Lake pool after renovations were completed. ***(Homewood-Flossmoor Park District)***

Independence Park, the village's tribute to the nation's bicentennial, was dedicated there in 1976.

Independence Park was just one of a number of projects the park district developed in the 1970s. In 1969, the independent park districts of Homewood and Flossmoor merged, allowing the combined

Homewood-Flossmoor Park District the ability to provide improved services and additional programs.

A year after the merger took place, the park district purchased the 8-1/2-acre Dolphin Lake property at the corner of 183rd Street and Governors Highway. This property originally had been built as an amenity for homeowners in the Dolphin Lake Estates subdivision. Once the park district acquired the property, the clubhouse, pool, and lake were immediately made available to district residents for swimming, fishing, boating, meetings, and other park programs.

Three years later, the park district completed construction of the Homewood-Flossmoor Racquet Club. This complex opened in January 1973 and featured eight indoor tennis courts, four racquetball/handball courts, a pro shop, an exercise room, locker rooms, a sauna, and a whirlpool. Early in 1975, the district completed the purchase of the Lions Club pool and the acreage that surrounded it, and in November 1975, the district opened the Homewood-Flossmoor Ice Arena on Kedzie Avenue. This facility boasted a 200' x 85' main ice rink with spectator stands capable of seating thirteen hundred people, a smaller studio rink for lessons and figure skating, a concessions stand, a pro shop, a skate rental and sharpening shop, and four large locker rooms. All of these facilities have since been enlarged and upgraded over the years, and they continue to provide first-class recreational opportunities for all district residents.

Homewood-Flossmoor Racquet Club ***(Homewood-Flossmoor Park District)***

Homewood-Flossmoor High School, in a classic example of intergovernmental cooperation, donated the land on which the ice arena was built. In exchange for the donation, the park district grants 540 hours of free ice time each year to the school, and H-F's hockey team has used the arena as their home rink since the facility was built. The high school, during its first decade, experienced tremendous growth. By 1970, the school's enrollment had grown to over 3,000 students who were forced to attend classes in two shifts because of overcrowding. To address this problem, a new building was built north of the main building on Governors Highway. The North building, with a capacity of 1,500 students, was completed in November 1971 and housed the freshman class. Enrollment at the high school continued to grow and reached 3,716 students in September 1972. By the end of the decade, this number had declined to 3,290 as the last of the baby boomers were completing high school.

North of the high school on Kedzie Avenue, another school, the Homewood Christian Academy, opened in 1976 offering instruction for students in kindergarten through twelfth grade. The academy, which now has an enrollment of about three hundred pupils, recently changed its name to the Homewood Community Academy and is affiliated with the All Nations Community Church, formerly known as the Homewood Full Gospel Church. The Homewood Full Gospel Church was organized in 1973, and services were initially held at Homewood-Flossmoor High School until the congregation's sanctuary was completed later that year at 18620 Kedzie Avenue.

Temple B'nai Yehuda was another congregation established in the village during this period to serve the needs of those of the Jewish faith in the Homewood area. The congregation, which was organized in 1944 in Hyde Park, later moved to Eighty-second Street and Jeffrey in South Shore before moving to Homewood. The congregation's first services in Homewood were held in 1969 at St. Andrew's Methodist Church. Construction of a new synagogue was completed in 1970 at 1424 183rd Street, and Rabbi Leo Wolkow, who had been associated with the synagogue since 1964, led the congregation until his retirement in 1998. That year, Ellen Dreyfus was elected rabbi, and B'nai Yehuda merged with Beth Sholom, a congregation from Park Forest. Since 1998, all activities for the new congregation, B'nai Yehuda Beth Sholom, have been consolidated in Homewood.

Perhaps one of the greatest changes in the 1960s and 1970s was the way people shopped. During this era, large shopping centers were being

Temple B'nai Yehuda as it looked in 1975

constructed throughout the area, and the term "mall" entered the nation's parlance. Shoppers flocked to new "plazas" and "malls" that offered a variety of stores that were conveniently located near one another and accessed through ample parking lots. Older retail districts in the downtowns of communities like Homewood and neighboring Harvey and Chicago Heights quickly began to feel the effects of this competition.

In the south suburbs, Evergreen Plaza at Ninety-fifth Street and Western Avenue was the area's first indoor mall, constructed in 1952. Following Evergreen Plaza, stores in Park Forest Plaza opened in phases from 1950 through the early 1960s. Dixie Square Mall in Harvey opened in 1966, River Oaks Shopping Center in Calumet City opened in 1967, and Lincoln Mall in Matteson and Orland Square Mall in Orland Park opened in 1973 and 1975, respectively.

Larger shopping venues were also being built in Homewood. Cherry Creek Shopping Center at 183rd Street and Governors Highway was completed in 1969 and was anchored by Dominick's Finer Foods, Walgreens Drug Store, Ben Franklin Store, Ace Hardware, and a number of smaller stores including Corky's Hamburgers, the Varsity Shop, Little Colony, and Edwin David clothing stores. Farther west on 183rd Street, a Jewel Food Store and the W. T. Grant Department Store were built in 1969 and 1971 just east of Kedzie Avenue.

Across town on Halsted Street, the 400,000-square-foot Washington Square Mall opened in 1974 just north of Ridge Road. The mall was anchored by the Diana Theatres, Robert Hall Village, Service Merchandise Catalog Showroom, Dominick's Finer Foods, Walgreens Drug Store, and a host of smaller stores including Frederick's of

Washington Square Mall on the east side of Halsted Street north of Ridge Road was completed in 1974.

Hollywood, Minnesota Fabrics, Kinney Shoes, Stuart's Fashions, and Brainerd Men's Wear, which moved from downtown Homewood to the mall location. In 1975, Washington Park Plaza opened across the road on the west side of Halsted Street and was anchored by the Woolco Department Store and a Jewel Food Store. Other tenants included Radio Shack, Cara Ann Casuals, and Alexander's Book Store.

Development also occurred on Halsted Street south of Ridge Road, which included the Bay Furniture Store, South End Savings and Loan, and the Sulky Club Restaurant. On the north end of Halsted, the five-story Sheraton Homewood Inn was built just north of the Washington Park Race Track and opened in 1975. In just a short period of time, Halsted Street had become the commercial hub of Homewood, and some businesses downtown began to suffer. Jewel Food Stores closed their location on Dixie Highway in 1976, and other stores, like the Ben Franklin on Ridge Road, followed suit.

As the 1970s drew to a close, development slowed since much of Homewood was already built up, with the exception of parcels of land east of Kedzie Avenue and south of 183rd Street and selected sites scattered around town. The village was also landlocked with no ability to annex adjacent territory. Homewood had matured although the conflagration that leveled the grandstand and clubhouse of Washington Park Race Track the night of February 5, 1977, cleared the way for the eventual redevelopment of over 350 acres of land, a process that still is not complete almost three decades later.

Washington Park Plaza, across Halsted Street from the mall, opened in 1975 and was anchored by Woolco and Jewel Food Store.

Flames devour the grandstand of Washington Park Race Track on February 5, 1977.

Smoldering ruins of the grandstand of Washington Park Race Track

CHAPTER 14
Homewood Lately

After fire destroyed the grandstand of Washington Park Race Track, the village was faced, at once, with a huge problem—the loss of its largest taxpayer—and a huge opportunity—the ability to redevelop the largest parcel of vacant land in the area. Homewood village officials worked diligently with the landowner, the Madison Square Garden Corporation, to come up with an acceptable plan to redevelop the site and to ultimately replace the property tax revenues the village lost when the building went up in flames. After two years of meetings, public hearings, and legal counseling, the village board approved a comprehensive redevelopment proposal for the site in the summer of 1979. This plan called for commercial, industrial, and office-research uses to be situated along Ashland Avenue and Halsted and 175th Streets and the addition of single and multifamily residences along the south and western perimeters of the parcel. At the time, Madison Square Garden Corporation also donated 10 percent of the land to the village for open space and use for municipal services as needed. This donation included a number of acres of prairie land.

As proposed, the development was to add twenty-five hundred residents to the village's population and was to provide hundreds of new jobs. The development was expected to increase the village's assessed valuation by \$114 million and was to pump over \$6 million of tax revenues into village coffers. Spirits and expectations were high, and the development was projected to be complete by 1985. This timetable seemed realistic considering no other site was available in such close proximity to the Tri-State Tollway and the network of superhighways, including I-80, I-94, and I-57, that Washington Park was near.

The Girl Scouts of America building on 175th Street was one of the first office buildings constructed on the former racetrack property. *(Carolyn Funk)*

By 1985, however, little had been accomplished. Office buildings built on 175th Street, including ones occupied by State Farm Insurance and the Girl Scouts of America, nibbled at the north edges of the property, and a string of eleven homes had been constructed on the southeastern corner of the site on a street called Presidents Drive. A sluggish economy, numerous changes in ownership of the land, and high commercial property taxes in Cook County were all blamed as impediments to development. Over the next few years, several more office buildings were built on 175th Street. A senior care facility was built on Maple Road; and Park Place Plaza, anchored by PharMor Discount Food and Drugstore, Silo Appliances, and Goldblatt's Department Store, was built on the east side of Halsted Street north of Washington Square Mall.

Frustrated by the slow pace of development on the west side of Halsted Street, the village negotiated the purchase of the remaining 178 acres of Washington Park Race Track land for $2.4 million in 1991. Now in complete control of the development, the village moved to reevaluate plans for the site, which, at one time, included proposals for everything from a music theatre and convention center complex, to a golf course, and even to construction of a sports stadium.

Homes on Presidents Drive were also built on the former racetrack grounds. Their rear yards now face Prairie Lakes. *(Carolyn Funk)*

The result of the village's efforts was the Prairie Lakes Business Park. Prairie Lakes was to offer a unique combination of public land, prairie preserve, wetlands, and recreational space surrounding corporate sites in a campus-like setting. Plans for the business park also included a network of three interconnected lakes covering over forty acres, which would provide a much-needed watershed for storm water runoff and flood control for areas in central Homewood, south and west of the development.

At the same time the plan for Prairie Lakes was evolving, the village was also negotiating with the Kmart Corporation to allow them to build a new Super Kmart and Builders Square II home improvement store south of 175th Street on the west side of Halsted Street. The company completed these stores in 1994 and vacated the space the stores previously occupied on the east side of Halsted Street in Washington Square Mall. Kmart had taken over the old Robert Hall Village site in the early 1980s while Builders Square moved into the building in 1986.

Builders Square completed this store on the west side of Halsted Street in 1994. ***(Village of Homewood)***

Since the plans for the Prairie Lakes Business Park were approved in 1995, development of the corporate sites has progressed to where more than 60 percent of the park is now complete. Lighting Distributors Incorporated was the first company to build in the park; Exhibit Source, Fiber Solutions, and Brudi Bolzoni Auramo, Inc., an Italian forklift manufacturer, followed them. Homewood Disposal has also received approval to build an office building on the site. Freedom Village, a multistory senior housing complex, occupies land in the southeast section of the park across from Heartland Healthcare Center on Maple Road. Aggressive marketing, tax incentives, and free land offered by the village, coupled with a beautiful setting, have all helped to speed the completion of this development.

Development of racetrack land was not the only issue facing village planners in the 1980s and 1990s. By the late 1970s, competition from businesses along the Halsted Street corridor and nearby malls had taken a toll on stores in the central business district, and many storefronts were left vacant. In addition, some buildings in the downtown

Exhibit Source is one of the companies that has completed a modern office and warehouse facility in Prairie Lakes Business Park. *(Carolyn Funk)*

area had fallen into disrepair, and the sidewalks and street lighting were in need of replacement. Like many other cities struggling with their aging downtowns and infrastructure needs, Homewood looked for a way to rejuvenate the area and a source of funding to do it. After considerable study, the village board voted to adopt a tax increment financing (TIF) plan in 1978. This option allowed the village to freeze tax assessments in the area downtown slated for redevelopment, and then use any additional tax revenues the redevelopment generated for public improvements. Homewood was the second community in Illinois to use this funding mechanism after the state passed the TIF law in 1977.

The initial phase of the downtown redevelopment plan called for extensive changes in an area generally centered on the intersection of Hickory Road and Martin Avenue. The village purchased a number of parcels on the two streets, and houses on them were burned down to make way for new development. Gone were the homes dating to the mid-to-late-nineteenth century of families like the Steiners, Rathjes and Grannises. In their place, private developers constructed the twenty-four-unit Martin Place condominium project, the Illinois Central Hospital Association office building, and another building on the west side of Martin Avenue that included commercial occupancies on the first floor and apartments on the second and third floors.

Tax dollars generated by these projects were then used to finance public improvements in the area. Utilities were installed underground, off-street parking lots were reconfigured and rebuilt to increase efficiency and capacity, curbs and streetlights

Ridge Road looking east from Harwood Avenue today. *(Village of Homewood/ Les Hier)*

were installed, and considerable landscaping was planted throughout the area. A unique part of the project was the facelift given to the rear of buildings that fronted the south side of Ridge Road.

Brick sidewalks and decorative lights along Ridge Road looking west from Gottschalk Avenue. *(Village of Homewood/ Les Hier)*

An unsightly hodgepodge of brick walls, some dating to the early 1900s, faced customers using the expanded parking lots behind the stores on the south side of Ridge Road between Harwood Avenue and Dixie Highway. To make this area more attractive, the village hired renowned artist Richard Haas who designed a series of *trompe l'oeil* (fool the eye) murals to beautify the rear façades of these stores. In essence, the Haas murals made the rear of the buildings look like they were actually the fronts.

Artist works on the Haas *trompe l'oeil* murals. *(Village of Homewood)*

The first phase of improvements downtown was completed in 1983, and once additional funding was available, a second phase of improvements began in 1992. This phase included streetscape improvements along Dixie Highway and Ridge Road in the central business district. New sidewalks, accented with brick pavers, were installed in this area along with street lighting reminiscent of the 1890s, benches, and planters landscaped with shrubbery and flowers. To further beautify the downtown, the village initiated a façade improvement program, which offered matching funds to business owners interested in renovating the exteriors of their buildings.

View looking southbound on Dixie Highway toward Ridge Road today *(Village of Homewood/ Les Hier)*

These programs have been a great success and have greatly enhanced the look of downtown Homewood. To further illustrate the success of these revitalization efforts, the village received a national award in 1993 for the façade program, and other communities in the Chicago area have copied both the façade and streetscape programs. In addition, the village has also extended participation to other areas in town and has completed streetscape improvements along Harwood Avenue and in the Southgate shopping district.

Dixie Highway at Ridge Road today *(Village of Homewood/ Les Hier)*

On the fringes of downtown, the school board, park district, and library were responsible for other developments that helped increase the viability and attractiveness of the center of town. By the early 1980s, the enrollment in School District 153 had fallen to about nineteen hundred students. The school district had plenty of capacity in each of its school buildings, and an economic decision was made to close Central School on Highland Avenue, the district's oldest building, constructed in 1923. The building and land were subsequently put up for sale.

View looking north on Dixie Highway from 183rd Street today *(Village of Homewood/ Les Hier)*

In February 1985, Richard D. Irwin, founder of the well-known college textbook publishing company bearing his name, donated $2.25 million to the Homewood-Flossmoor Park District to enable them to buy the school property and complete the construction of a new community center on it. Irwin, a local benefactor for many years, established his company in 1933 with offices in Chicago. In 1951, Irwin moved the company headquarters to Homewood in an attractive new building built at 1818 Ridge Road. The company expanded, and the American Legion building on the northwest corner of Ridge Road and Highland Avenue was purchased, torn down, and a two-story addition was added to the original Irwin building. As the company continued to grow and prosper, a second building was built on the northwest corner of Ridge Road and Homewood Avenue. Irwin sold the firm to the Dow Jones Company in 1975, and they later sold it to the Times-Mirror Publishing Company in 1988. Times-Mirror closed the Homewood offices and moved to new facilities in Burr Ridge in 1994.

Through the years that the Irwin Company was in Homewood, Mr. Irwin enjoyed seeing children play in the schoolyard across the street from his office. The desire to see this tradition continue led him to make his donation to the park district. Construction of the community center, named in honor of his wife Marie, began in November 1985 and was completed the next year. The 26,000-square-foot building immediately became, and continues to be, the focal point for park programs for young and old alike. The band shell on the west side of the building also serves as a popular venue for concerts and other entertaining acts throughout the summer months, and the parkland adjacent to the band shell provides a perfect spot to view these acts.

A year after the Irwin Center opened, the school board decided to sell Ridge School located on Gottschalk Avenue south of Ridge Road. Bids were accepted, and the two highest bidders were the park district and the Homewood Library. The park district's bid of $250,000 was the highest by $10,000, and after they acquired the site, it was converted to parkland complete with a playground, gazebo, and beautiful fountain. The only parcel in the block between Highland and Gottschalk Avenues on Ridge Road that the park district did not own was the site on which the old telephone exchange building, built in 1927, was located. The district purchased this site and demolished the building to complete the park in 1999. That same year, the district also began work converting the old Hines Lumber Yard on Harwood Avenue into Millennium Park and the former Army Nike radar base on 187th Street into Patriot's Park.

Groundbreaking ceremonies for the Marie Irwin Community Center. From left are Homewood Village President Manny Hoffman, Richard Irwin, Marie Irwin, Park President Jack Fitzer, and Flossmoor Village President Bert Reed. *(Homewood-Flossmoor Park District)*

The library had an interest in the Ridge School property as a potential site for a new building. In the years since the library was completed on Dixie Highway in 1962, the increasing demands for services and their expanded collections had outgrown the facility. After being

Residents line up for tours of the Marie Irwin Community Center, September 24, 1986. *(Homewood-Flossmoor Park District)*

outbid on the Ridge School property, the library board was able to purchase an abandoned gas station at 17911 Dixie Highway, across the street from their existing site, in the fall of 1987. Later that year, voters approved the sale of $2.9 million in bonds to finance the construction of a new building. The 41,500-square-foot structure was completed in 1990, and, in a move reminiscent of the one the library made some thirty years before, patrons were encouraged to take out ten books in the weeks before the move and return them to the new library after it opened. The encouragement worked, thus easing the logistics and expense of the move.

View of the fountain in Richard D. Irwin Park. ***(Village of Homewood/ Les Hier)***

Overall view of Irwin Park. Central School was torn down to make room for the park. The school's limestone name panel was saved and is now used as a bench. ***(Village of Homewood/ Les Hier)***

Several blocks south of the library, the village was attempting to ignite the reuse of the shuttered Homewood Theatre. Closed in 1984, the vacant theatre was eyed as a potential location for a performing arts center. In 1986, the village purchased the building, and a year later, the Homewood Cultural Arts Center Foundation was established to raise funds and coordinate the refurbishment of the building, which was estimated to cost about $500,000. Like many remodeling projects, the fifty-year-old theatre was found to be in far worse condition than initially thought, and by 1990, the plan switched from refurbishing the building to reconstructing an entirely new building on the site incorporating the Art Deco elements of the original theatre structure.

Despite raising hundreds of thousands of dollars and securing the support of many in Homewood and the surrounding south suburban area, the Cultural Arts Foundation was forced to abandon its plans

when the costs to build a new building were projected to exceed $1 million. The curtain dropped at the Homewood Theatre for the last time in March 1992 as wreckers made quick work at demolishing the structure. Today, the site is a municipal parking lot.

A desire to preserve Homewood's heritage and prevent the destruction of landmarks like the Homewood Theatre and so many other buildings torn or burned down in the previous decades led a group of determined residents to organize the Homewood Historical Society in 1980. Co-founded by Jerry and Elaine Egdorf and Frank and Barbara Vodvarka, the society was organized with forty-seven charter members; Elaine Egdorf served as its first president. Today, the organization's membership hovers around three hundred.

The Homewood Public Library building was completed in 1990. ***(Joann Hibbins)***

Haas mural on the rear of the Homewood Theatre on Dixie Highway. ***(William F. Moore)***

Armed with the goal to preserve local history in the form of documents, photographs, and other memorabilia, the budding historians were presented with their greatest challenge shortly after organizing. Widow Hertha Howe, who owned and lived in one of the "HOME-

Demolition of the Homewood Theatre in 1992. The site is now a municipal parking lot. *(William F. Moore)*

WOOD" brick homes that Henry Gottschalk had built in 1891, was in the process of selling her home at 2035 183rd Street to the Homewood Federal Savings and Loan, whose building occupied the lot adjacent to the house. The savings and loan had planned on demolishing the structure to enlarge its parking lot. In February 1981, Mrs. Howe offered the house and contents to the society if members wanted it, but time was short. The bank was to close on the property in weeks.

At the instigation of the historical society, the village adopted a historic landmarks ordinance later in 1981, and the Howe house and the former home of Henry Gottschalk on Martin Avenue were named as the village's first two landmarks. The Howe house was saved from imminent destruction, but the savings and loan had since taken possession of the property. The house was not completely safe from destruction.

Below: The Homewood Historical Society's Dorband-Howe House Museum.

The Gottschalk House today at 18101 Martin Avenue. ***(Carolyn Funk)***

After a lengthy process, which took several years, the society worked out an agreement in 1985 with the savings and loan that allowed the bank to tear down the barn at the rear of the property for more parking so the house could remain. The savings and loan then gave the house to the village, which leases it to the historical society for $1 per year.

After this deal was finalized, society members worked nights and weekends restoring the home inside and out. Grand opening ceremonies for the refurbished Dorband-Howe House Museum, named for the two families who lived in the home the longest, took place on June 28, 1987. Today, the home continues to serve as the society's headquarters and museum, and it houses a large collection of artifacts, photos, and documents relating to the village's history. In addition to the museum, the society has made an impact on the village in other areas including sponsoring the placement of plaques on a number of historic sites and buildings throughout downtown Homewood.

By the mid-1990s, the investment of groups like the historical society, the village, and independent business owners had brought Homewood's downtown area back to a vibrant and thriving business center. As luck would have it, the fortunes of many of the businesses along the Halsted Street corridor did not fare as well during this same period.

Jewel Food Store on Halsted Street was completed in 2000. ***(Carolyn Funk)***

The Washington Square Mall was one of these businesses. During much of its existence, the mall struggled to survive in a competitive environment dominated by the larger regional malls in the area, including Orland Square in Orland Park,

Lincoln Mall in Matteson, and River Oaks in Calumet City. By the mid-1990s, the departure of the Diana Theatres, the Walgreens Drug Store to a new building on 183rd Street, the Builders Square to a new building across the street from the mall, and the exodus of other smaller tenants had made it difficult for the mall to survive. The mall closed, and the building was demolished in 1998 to allow room for the construction of a Home Depot home improvement store, which opened in the spring of 1999. A new Jewel Food Store, along with an Office Max and other smaller stores, was built north of the Home Depot on the former mall property and opened in the spring of 2000.

Target Department Store on Halsted Street was completed in 2002. ***(Carolyn Funk)***

The demolition of the twenty-four-year-old mall took place on the heels of the demolition of the former Silo and PharMor Stores built north of the mall in the mid-1980s. Both of these retail chains had gone bankrupt and were forced to close their Homewood stores. Menard's, another home improvement retailer like Home Depot, bought the property on which these stores were located and built a new store there in 1995. South of Menard's, the remaining stores of the Park Place Plaza, including Goldblatt's and Joann Fabrics, were demolished in 2001 to allow for the construction of a new Target Department Store. In a short span of time, the east side of Halsted Street was transformed from a strip dominated by an ailing mall to one populated by a number of national "big box" retailers.

The west side of Halsted Street has been a somewhat different story. The bankruptcy of the Venture Department Store chain led them to close their store in Homewood in 1998. The Venture had taken over the space Woolco had vacated in the early 1980s. The departure of the Venture left a big gap in the twenty-three-year-old Washington Park Plaza, which was made even larger when the other major tenant in the plaza, the Jewel Food Store, moved to the east side of Halsted Street. Redevelopment of Washington Park Plaza is still a major emphasis of the village's board and economic development staff.

While the rise and fall and rise again of the village's commercial areas were a major part of the last twenty years, Homewood continued to provide first-class educational, recreational, and municipal services despite these economic uncertainties. The levels of services provided are without peer in the area, and the village prides itself on being the "jewel" of the southern suburbs. These proclamations are more than just the boasts of overexuberant civic boosters; they are backed up by the awards to prove them. Over the last twenty years, Homewood schools, parks, and the village itself have won a number of awards bestowed by a variety of organizations, attesting to the high quality of life and services provided to the residents of the community.

The park district's Lions Club pool and waterslide as it looks today *(Village of Homewood/ Les Hier)*

The United States Department of Education gives its Blue Ribbon Award only to elementary and high schools in the country that exhibit the highest degree of excellence in educating their students. Homewood's Churchill School won the award in 1986, and James Hart

Homewood Izaak Walton President Robert Ahlf, Village President Manny Hoffman, and "Save the Prairie" coordinator Mary Murdoch on the south lawn of the White House for Take Pride in America ceremonies

Vice President George Bush addresses crowds at Ridge Road and Dixie Highway during his presidential campaign in 1988. Homewood Village President Manny Hoffman stands next to him as Fire Chief Joseph Klauk looks on. *(Chicago Heights Library)*

Junior High School won the award in 1997. Homewood-Flossmoor High School, exemplifying its long traditions of quality education, won the award on three separate occasions. The school is one of only two high schools in Illinois and twenty-five nationwide to have achieved this recognition three times. Homewood-Flossmoor won their first Blue Ribbon Award in 1983, followed by the second in 1996, and the third in 2002.

The Homewood-Flossmoor Park District is also an award-winning institution, garnering the National Recreation and Parks Association's Gold Medal Award in 1991. This award is the most prestigious honor bestowed on any park and recreation agency in the United States. The park district also received the Illinois Parks and Recreation Association's Distinguished Agency Award in 1997.

In addition to fine schools and parks, the village is renowned for its superb level of municipal services and high quality of life. Homewood has been voted the top community in the Chicago Southland by readers of the *Star Newspaper* three years in a row from

1994 to 1996 and yearly since 1999. *Chicago Magazine* has also ranked the village top in its category in community surveys the magazine conducted in 1996 and 2002.

Recognition of Homewood as a quality community also reached presidential levels.

President Ronald Reagan recognized the community's efforts, led by the Homewood Izaak Walton Chapter, in raising $400,000 through grants, donations, and other fundraising activities to purchase nine acres of native prairie land threatened with development on the former Washington Park property. The Izaak Walton Chapter spearheaded the successful "Save the Prairie" campaign, which culminated in the purchase of the property in 1984. The campaign and subsequent prairie management efforts, all done by volunteer labor, caught the attention of the White House and Reagan, who presented a delegation from Homewood with a Take Pride in America Award in the Rose Garden in July 1987.

The following year, Vice President George Bush visited the community during his presidential campaign, stopping at the corner of Ridge Road and Dixie Highway to greet enthusiastic crowds. Bush and muscleman-turned-actor, and now governor, Arnold Schwarzenegger even had lunch at the Three Brothers Restaurant at the intersection of Ridge Road and Dixie Highway for the quintessential small town photo opportunity.

Vice President George Bush talks with Homewood Village President Manny Hoffman and Arnold Schwarzenegger at the counter of Three Brothers Restaurant. ***(Chicago Heights Library)***

In 1996, President Bill Clinton chose Blue Ribbon Award–winning Homewood-Flossmoor High School as a stop on his campaign trail. Clinton visited the school on September 17, and a crowd estimated at over twenty-five thousand people turned out to greet him. Clinton was introduced to the crowd by the school's student body president and Homewood resident Brendan Cumiskey.

Presidents Clinton, Bush, and Reagan, like countless numbers of more common folk, have all helped to weave the fabric of Homewood through the years. Today, over 170 years after the first settlers arrived in our area, Homewood remains a great place to grow up, raise a family, and live—a beloved hometown that generations call "home sweet home."

Homewood-Flossmoor High School Superintendent Laura Murray cheers with the crowd while student body president Brendan Cumiskey and President Bill Clinton look on. *(Homewood-Flossmoor High School)*

BIBLIOGRAPHY

Chapter 1

Ahlf, Robert, et al. *Izaak Walton Preserve, A History Revised and Updated.* Homewood, 1993

Andreas, Alfred T. *History of Cook County, Illinois.* Chicago, 1884

Corliss, Carlton. *Trails to Rails: A Story of Transportation Progress in Illinois.* Illinois Central Railroad, 1937

Illinois State Archives Online Database of Public Land Sales Records

Indiana Dunes National Lakeshore Bailly Homestead. <http://www.savedunes.org/html/bailly.html>

Kuch, Margaret. *James Hart, Legend and Fact.* Homewood Historical Society, 1989

———. *Key to the Past.* Homewood Historical Society, 1996

Michalek, Louise. *A Look into the Past: Chicago Heights and Her Neighbors.* Chicago Heights, 1961

Milne, Muriel Mueller. *Our Roots Are Deep; A History of Monee, Illinois.* Monee, 1973

Spooner, A. L. "The Bailly Trading Post." *Newaygo County Historical Archives.* <http://ncha.ncats.net/html/index.html>

United States Bureau of Land Management, General Land Office Records Online Database

Chapter 2

Andreas, Alfred T. *History of Cook County, Illinois.* Chicago, 1884

Corliss, Carlton. *Trails to Rails: A Story of Transportation Progress in Illinois.* Illinois Central Railroad, 1937

Heimburger, Donald. *Illinois Central: Main Line of Mid-America.* Heimburger House Publishing, 1995

"Homewood Noted for Golf, Races and Fine Homes." *Hammond Times,* 1 May 1940

Illinois Central Railroad Company. *Annual Reports.* 1855–1859

Kuch, Margaret. *James Hart, Legend and Fact.* Homewood Historical Society, 1989

———. *Key to the Past.* Homewood Historical Society, 1996

"Mrs. Wm. Doepp, 87, Pioneer, Dead." *Homewood News,* 8 March 1928

100th Anniversary of the First Presbyterian Church. Homewood, 1958

Schapper, Ferdinand. *Southern Cook County Before the Civil War.* Chicago Historical Society, 1917

Chapter 3

Adair, Anna, and Adele Sandberg. *Indian Trails to Tollways.* Harvey: Fremouw Press, 1968

Andreas, Alfred T. *History of Cook County, Illinois.* Chicago, 1884

Corliss, Carlton. *Trails to Rails: A Story of Transportation Progress in Illinois.* Illinois Central Railroad, 1937

Hinko, Michael. *History of Homewood.* Homewood: Richard D. Irwin, 1976

Homewood Village Board of Trustees Minutes, November 1924

Illinois Central Railroad Company. *Organization and Traffic of the Illinois Central System.* 1938

Illinois State Archives Online Database of Civil War Veterans

Kuch, Margaret. *Key to the Past.* Homewood Historical Society, 1996

McClellan, Dr. Larry. *St. Paul Church 135 Years of Worship, Fellowship and Service.* Homewood, 2000

Reece, J. N. *Report of the Adjutant General of the State of Illinois.* Springfield, 1900

Sullivan, Michael. *History of Homewood Post 483, American Legion.* Homewood, 1941

Chapter 4

"A Busy Man of the Old Days." *Homewood News,* 22 March 1928

Dillon, Beulah. *A Brief History of the Homewood Public Schools.* Homewood, 1980

Goodspeed, W. A. *History of Cook County, Illinois.* Chicago, 1909

"Henry Stolzenbach Dies at 80 Years, Village Treasurer." *Chicago Heights Star,* 5 January 1937

"A Homewood Thanksgiving Way Back When as told by Henry Gottschalk." *Homewood News,* 29 November 1929

"How Homewood Got Its Name." *Homewood News,* 15 March 1928

Illinois Central Railroad Company. *Guide to Illinois Central Lands.* Chicago, 1867

"Main Street in the Old Days." *Homewood News,* 5 April 1928

"Old Settlers Corner: Interview with Carl Steiner." *Homewood News,* 27 June 1929

United States Census Records 1860, 1870, and 1880

Chapter 5

"A Busy Man of the Old Days." *Homewood News,* 22 March 1928

"First Village Board Who They Were and What They Did." *Homewood News,* 8 March 1928

"A Homewood Thanksgiving Way Back When as told by Henry Gottschalk." *Homewood News,* 29 November 1929

Homewood Village Board of Trustees Minutes 1893–1900

"Rough House at Homewood—22 Young Harvey Men Arrested." *Harvey Tribune,* September 1904

"Two Women & A Child Killed—Struck by the Big Four Express." *Chicago Daily Tribune,* 12 December 1891

Chapter 6

Adair, Anna, and Adele Sandberg. *Indian Trails to Tollways.* Harvey: Fremouw Press, 1968

Central Electric Railfan's Association. *Trolley Sparks Bulletin 93,* February 1951

Chicago Heights Star, 1906–1910 editions

Dillon, Beulah. *A Brief History of the Homewood Public Schools.* Homewood, 1980

Dolton-Riverdale Pointer, 1906–1910 editions

Harvey Tribune, 1900–1910 editions

Hinko, Michael. *History of Homewood.* Homewood: Richard D. Irwin, 1976

Homewood Board of Local Improvements Minutes 1900–1911

Homewood Village Board of Trustees Minutes 1900–1911

Chapter 7

Adair, Anna, and Adele Sandberg. *Indian Trails to Tollways.* Harvey: Fremouw Press, 1968

"Calumet C.C. Centennial." *Chicago District Golfer,* November/December 2001

"Dixmoor Golf Club—The 6th Club Located in This Vicinity." *Harvey Tribune,* 2 December 1921

Georgiady, Peter. *North American Club Makers.* Kernersville, N.C.: Airlie Hall Press, 1998

Graffis, Herbert B. *The PGA: The Official History of the Professional Golfers Association of America.* New York: Crowell, 1975

Idlewild Country Club. *First Annual Report to the Board of Directors,* 1909

"John F. Gilchrist Tells How Flossmoor Country Club Started." *Homewood News,* 8 November 1929

"Latest Addition to the Golf Club Colony Served by the Illinois Central." *Illinois Central Magazine,* July 1921

Ravisloe Country Club Twenty-Fifth Anniversary. Homewood, 1926

Thomas, Ruth. *The Tradition Endures: Flossmoor Country Club, 1899–1999.* Flossmoor, 1999

Chapter 8

Chicago Heights Star, 1911–1919 editions

Dolton-Riverdale Pointer, 1911–1919 editions

Harvey Tribune, 1911–1919 editions

History of St. Joseph's Parish. Homewood, 1987

Homewood Village Board of Trustees Minutes 1911–1919

Kuch, Margaret. *75 Years of God's Grace—Salem Lutheran Church 1919–1994.* Homewood, 1994

100th Anniversary of the First Presbyterian Church. Homewood, 1958

Sullivan, Michael. *History of Homewood Post 483, American Legion.* Homewood, 1941

Chapter 9

Chicago Heights Star, 1920–1929 editions

Dillon, Beulah. *A Brief History of the Homewood Public Schools.* Homewood, 1980

"Electric Service Is Acclaimed." *Illinois Central Magazine,* September 1926

Homewood Directory. Chicago: McDonough and Company, 1927 & 1930

Homewood News, 1925–1929 editions

Homewood Village Board of Trustees Minutes 1920–1929

"Improvements Making Progress." *Illinois Central Magazine,* September 1925

"Markham Yards Open to Full Use." *Illinois Central Magazine,* April 1926

Neutrowound Radio Manufacturing Company. *Super Power Radio Station WOK.* Homewood, 1927

"Progress in Our Terminal Electrification." *Illinois Central Magazine,* December 1922

"Shotgun Murder of Man and Woman Traced to Booze War." *Chicago Tribune,* 3 June 1926

"Survey Says 1929 Rich in Promise." *South Cook Courier,* 3 January 1929

"Will Push Markham Yards Work This Year." *Illinois Central Magazine,* March 1923

Chapter 10

Chicago Heights Star, 1930–1939 editions

"Homewood Noted for Golf, Races and Fine Homes." *Hammond Times,* 1 May 1940

"Homewood Postal Bandits Get $6,542.24." *South Cook Courier,* 24 April 1930

Homewood Village Board of Trustees Minutes 1930–1939

Chapter 11

Adair, Anna, and Adele Sandberg. *Indian Trails to Tollways*. Harvey: Fremouw Press, 1968

Ahlf, Robert, et al. *Izaak Walton Preserve, A History Revised and Updated.* Homewood, 1993

Chicago Heights Star/Homewood-Flossmoor Star, 1940–1949 editions

Homewood Village Board of Trustees Minutes 1940–1949

Chapter 12

Adair, Anna, and Adele Sandberg. *Indian Trails to Tollways*. Harvey: Fremouw Press, 1968

Dillon, Beulah. *A Brief History of the Homewood Public Schools*. Homewood, 1980

Homewood-Flossmoor League of Women Voters. *Presenting Homewood and Flossmoor.* Harvey: Fremouw Press, 1958

Homewood-Flossmoor Star, 1950–1959 editions

Homewood Review, 1951–1957 editions

United States Census Records 1950 & 1960

Village of Homewood. *Homewood's Year of Greatest Progress 1955–1956 Annual Report*. 1956

Chapter 13

Hometown: Homewood-Flossmoor. *Chicago Sun-Times*, August 1988

Homewood-Flossmoor Star, 1960–1979 editions

Homewood-Flossmoor Supplement. *Chicago Tribune*, 29 February 1984, section 8

Homewood-Flossmoor Supplement. *Chicago Tribune*, 6 March 1991, section 8

Homewood-Flossmoor Supplement. *Chicago Tribune*, 14 October 1987, section 8

Homewood-Flossmoor Supplement. *Suburban Tribune*, 20 June 1979

Homewood Police Department 1893–1968. Homewood, 1968

Profile: Homewood-Flossmoor. *Chicago Sun-Times*, January 1990

United States Census Records 1970 & 1980

Chapter 14

Adair, Anna, and Adele Sandberg. *Indian Trails to Tollways*. Harvey: Fremouw Press, 1968

Ahlf, Robert, et al. *Izaak Walton Preserve, A History Revised and Updated.* Homewood, 1993

Hometown: Homewood-Flossmoor. *Chicago Sun-Times*, August 1988

Homewood-Flossmoor Star, 1980–2003 editions

Homewood-Flossmoor Supplement. *Chicago Tribune*, 29 February 1984, section 8

Homewood-Flossmoor Supplement. *Chicago Tribune*, 6 March 1991, section 8

Homewood-Flossmoor Supplement. *Chicago Tribune*, 14 October 1987, section 8

Homewood-Flossmoor Supplement. *Suburban Tribune*, 20 June 1979

Profile: Homewood-Flossmoor. *Chicago Sun-Times*, January 1990

INDEX

C

D

E

F

G

H

I

J

N

O

S

T

U

V

ABOUT THE AUTHOR

(Photo by Frank Casella)

Jim Wright, a lifelong resident of Homewood, has had a keen interest in history, particularly Homewood history, since childhood.

A member of the Homewood Historical Society for over twenty years, Jim currently serves as the society's vice president and has served several terms as the organization's president. He has written extensively on the history of Homewood and has authored a book on the history of the Homewood Fire Department, which has been revised and updated and is currently in its third printing. In addition to his historical activities, Jim served twenty-two years as a member of the Homewood Fire Department and also served four years as an elected trustee on the Homewood Village Board, where he spearheaded efforts to preserve and restore Homewood's Depression-era Art Deco municipal building.

Professionally, Jim works as a supervisor for an insurance claims management company.

SINCLAIR
H-C
GASOLINE
DINO says
PEP!
POWER-X
MILEAGE!
Buy